PULLMAN CARS
ON THE "SOUTHERN"
1875–1972

by

R. W. Kidner

THE OAKWOOD PRESS

© The Oakwood Press 1987

ISBN 0 85361 356 7

Set by Gem Publishing Company, Brightwell, Wallingford, Oxon
Printed by S&S Press, Abingdon, Oxford

Author's Note

My interest in Pullman cars began sixty years ago when, during
walks around the Chislehurst area, I saw the rakes of red Pullmans
passing along the main line on their Continental occasions. No
literature on the subject existed at the time, so I made my own list. As
it turns out it was not quite complete; taking names of single cars was
no problem, but I once came across a train of red Pullmans in full
gallop for Folkestone Races, and only the fact that they all had short
names like *Mabel* and *Dora* saved the day. Over the years I have
watched and travelled in Pullmans, and my first sight of the
"Brighton Belle" in grey/blue livery was, I suppose, one of the sad-
dest occasions of what seems to my generation a great decline in
railway quality.

From 1888 when the Midland Railway contract ceased, up to 1960
when the "Blue Pullman" started running, most activity was on
Southern lines. There were cars working on other railways, but the
story of the company in its independent years is very much tied to the
Southern. For this reason, although there have been two excellent
books on Pullmans published in recent years, I felt there was room for
one which dealt in detail with this odd co-habitation of the Pullman
Company and the railways which made up the Southern Region of
BR.

March 1987   *R.W.K.*

Published by
The OAKWOOD PRESS
P.O.Box 122, Headington, Oxford.

Pullman Cars on the "Southern"

Contents

The "SOUTHERN BELLE"

CAR T. C. No. 88. | RESERVED 5.25pm SEAT No. **25**

Date 1st January, 1933 Train

The "SOUTHERN BELLE"

CAR T. C. No. 88. | RESERVED 5.25pm SEAT No. **26**

Date 1st January, 1933 Train

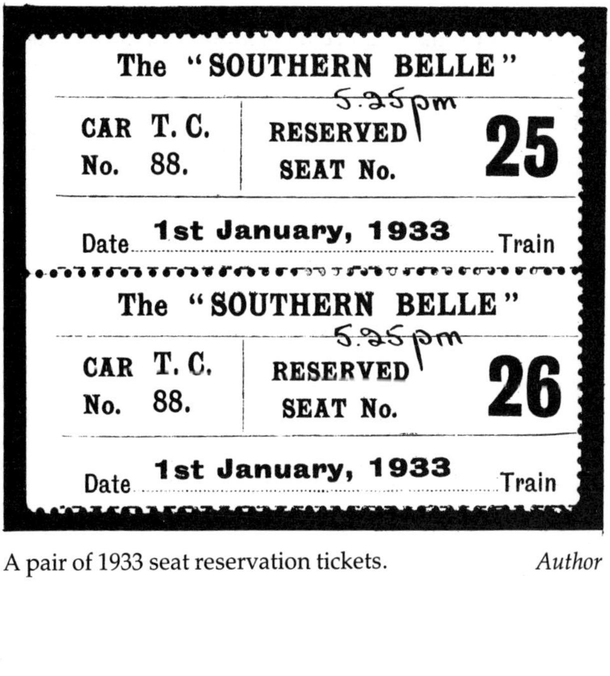

A pair of 1933 seat reservation tickets.   *Author*

Advertisement from *Railway Year Book*, 1924.

Chapter One

The Pullman Idea

A stranger seeing a Brighton express at the turn of the century, and noting one or two large American saloons sailing along in the middle of what were mostly six-wheeled carriages, might have wondered what they were doing there. The Pullman car, which ran in its own livery and did not belong to the railway, was certainly an anomaly, though it must be added that at that time most of the goods wagons did not belong to the railways either. It is perhaps surprising that the relationship with the operators, at any rate on the Southern lines, was so harmonious.

George Mortimer Pullman had been building his cars in the USA from the 1860s; they were nothing strange there, being similar to other stock, though offering sleeping and dining facilities. In Britain sleeping cars had been tried, but did not catch on; distances were mostly too short. On the continent of Europe there was more scope, and a company, titled the Compagnie Internationale des Wagons-Lits, had been set up in Belgium in 1872. Pullman also had his eye in that market, and Britain; he first found a partner in the Midland Railway, which was willing to assemble American-made saloons at the Derby works, and to run them in some trains. The first such train ran on 1st June, 1874. They were either sleeping cars or day drawing room cars; diners did not come in until 1879, when Pullman provided one for the Great Northern Railway. Between 1883 and 1888 when their Agreement expired, the MR bought up some Pullmans and operated them in its own livery; others were transferred to the London Brighton & South Coast Railway. The few GNR cars were also sold by 1895.

Pullman had certainly forced the railway companies to accept that they must provide dining and sleeping facilities, though this bene-fited him little and Pullman never again became involved in the UK with sleeping cars. However, the "Pullman Idea" was not really about eating and sleeping; it was about providing luxury travel above the ordinary first class, and seen to be so by its livery and décor. The company was to provide cars and service of a quality that the railways could not. A few railways accepted this idea, most at that time did not. However, such was the dedication of the management and staff of Pullman that in due course the idea of "Pullman and Perfection" was created in the public mind, leading to their later adoption on many main lines.

The British Pullman Car Company was formed in 1882, reformed with new management in 1908 and 1915, and then changed little until

1954 when the British Transport Commission started buying up the shares; by January 1963 it was a wholly-owned subsidiary, and later simply part of a Division of British Rail. By that time most of the glamour had gone; there were still privileged rail travellers, but they were mostly businessmen or officials for whom speed meant more than luxury. Real prestige now lay with the private aircraft. The "Pullman Idea" dwindled; however comfortable a carriage, if station premises are dirty and staff surly, the contentment of Pullman travel cannot be there. Yet the magic of the name did not die; it was kept going by the preserved Pullman trains described later.

The operational history of Pullman, especially on the Southern lines, is very complex and will be covered in later chapters; however, some general notes on the cars themselves will be of interest and are set out in the following chapter.

Chapter Two
Building, Naming, Numbering

Pullman cars were at first manufactured in the USA and assembled at a works set up by the Midland Railway at Derby; after 1888 and until a facility was set up at the former London Chatham & Dover works at Longhedge, assembly was carried out by the LBSCR at Brighton. However, from 1908 most cars were built by UK carriage building firms, Metropolitan, Birmingham, Cravens and Clayton. In 1928 rebuilding work was transferred from Longhedge to a large depot at Preston Park near Brighton.

Because they were built in small batches and for differing purposes, there was in the early days little standardisation. There were also frequent rebuildings and conversions as between parlour, kitchen and brake cars. However, some generalisations are possible: from 1874 to 1895 cars were entirely of wood and ran on four-wheeled bogies of American pattern, roofs being of the clerestory type sloping down at the ends; from 1899 to 1906 they were similar but ran on six-wheeled bogies. From 1908, when cars began to be built in the UK, they ceased to have clerestory roofs; from 1910 to 1914 they were mixed eight-wheeled and twelve-wheeled and had steel frames. No twelve-wheelers were built after 1923; from 1928 steel bodies were used.

The 1932 cars for electric sets were little changed in appearance though with a new design of bogie. Now for 19 years the Slump, the War, and post-War shortages meant that no new Pullmans were built. When some did appear in 1951 the only noticeable change was the use of square lavatory windows in place of the oval ones which had been a feature since 1906. These were the last cars built for the SR; in 1960 some new Pullmans were built for the ER East Coast services, but BR Mk 1 body shells were used; thereafter all new Pullmans were multiple-unit and owed nothing to previous practice.

There were seven main types of car arrangement: parlour cars with seating only, all-first class until 1915; kitchen cars with either 1st or 3rd class seating; bar cars classed or unclassed; composite cars with both 1st and 3rd class seating; brake cars with about one third given over to luggage space; guard cars with only a seat in one end vestibule; and observation cars of which there were only three, one in Scotland and two on the SR.

The relative requirements of these types of cars varied as contracts or services changed. Some rebuildings were so drastic that one could only take the company's word that it was the same car. In a few cases alterations were to improve exterior styling, as when *Albert Edward* had sixteen small windows altered to eight large ones. The largest number of rebuildings were to provide "end cars". Although the 1881 "Brighton Limited" had a baggage car, this idea was not continued, as it was expected that most Pullmans would work within trains; it was when all-Pullman trains became popular that end-cars with room for guard and luggage were called for. This did not apply to the "White Pullman" on the former SECR in 1924, where most of the baggage was sent in custom-sealed boxes on flat wagons, or with the following train, and for this "guard" cars were created, difficult to recognise as they only differed from parlour cars in having the word "guard" on one end door.

Dimensions

A casual scanning of published dimensions of Pullman cars can be very confusing, because it is seldom made clear whether the figure refers to "over body corners", "over vestibules" or "over buffers". In the early days of open platforms, it was natural to measure between the corner posts of the main body, as this was the useful part for accommodation. However, the platforms added some 6 feet, and buffers another 2–2½ feet, so that a "51 ft car" would be about 59½ ft over buffers. The early cars do not seem to have had a standard length; *Alexandra* was 54 ft "over sills" and 61 ft 0¾ in. over buffers. *Albert Edward* of the same year was 52 ft over sills and 59 ft 0¾ in. over buffers. *The Arundel*, an American-built twelve-wheeler of 1899, was 57 ft "over corners", 64 ft over vestibules and 65 ft 8 in. overall. The interior dimensions were made up of a 5 ft anteroom with ladies' WC,

31 ft 2 in. main saloon, 5 ft 6 in. anteroom with gents' WC and buffet, 6 ft 6 in. coupé, and 8 ft 6 in. small saloon. The insides of later cars were less complex. An article in the *Locomotive Magazine* stated that Pullmans were 58 ft up to 1894, then 61 ft to 1899, and 64 ft after that; these seem to be approximate lengths over vestibules. The height of the early clerestory-roofed cars was 13 ft. Bogie wheelbases were 8 ft until 1951 (12 ft for 6-wheel bogies) and 8 ft 6 in. after, but there were exceptions: the converted LNW cars of 1921 had 9 ft bogies and the LNER all-steel 1928 stock, 10 ft bogies.

Some comparative figures for main dimensions:

	Length over corners	Length over buffers	Height	Width	Weight
Maud 1877	52 ft	59 ft 5 in.	13 ft 2 in.	8 ft 11 in.	27 tons
1906 12-wheel	57 ft	65 ft 9 in.	13 ft 0 in.	8 ft 8¾ in.	35 tons
"Southern Belle" 1908	57 ft	65 ft 4 in.	13 ft 6 in.	8 ft 8¾ in.	40 tons
SECR 1910–14	51 ft	60 ft 0 in.	12 ft 6¾ in.	8 ft 7 in.	31–34 tons
Ex-GER 1920 12 w.	–	66 ft 11½ in.	12 ft 6 in.	8 ft 10 in.	43 tons
Ex-LNWR 1921	56 ft 9 in.	61 ft 0 in.	12 ft 6½ in	8 ft 7 in.	32 tons
Hastings cars 1926	–	–	12 ft 6 in.	8 ft 1 in.	38 tons
All-steel 1928	–	65 ft 10 in.	12 ft 5 in.	8 ft 7 in.	37–41 tons
6 PUL elec. 1932	59 ft 2½ in.	68 ft 8¾ in.	12 ft 5 in.	8 ft 11½ in.	43 tons
"Golden Arrow" 1951	–	65 ft 10 in.	12 ft 5 in.	8 ft 5½ in.	40–41 tons

The weights of the "Southern Belle" cars were: motor brakes 62 tons, 1st buffets 43 tons, 3rd parlours 40 tons. The overall length of the set was given officially as 335 ft. However, this assumes the buffers in a considerable state of compression, as the trailer cars had a length between vestibule plates of 66 ft and the motor cars were 66 ft 8¾ in. from the nose of the driving cab to the rear vestibule plate.

Seating Capacity

Pullman cars provided less seating capacity than normal carriages; in terms of tare weight, around 1¼ tons per passenger. The supplement went to Pullman so did not compensate the railway for carrying this deadweight; however, it must be remembered that the seat occupancy of Pullmans was higher than in normal carriages; on some services up to 100% day after day. In the early cars the seats were distributed sparsely to give an impression of a lounge; thus the parlour car *Princess* had 27 seats, the buffet car *Prince* 26, but the smoking car *Albert Victor*, which was not lounge-like, took 40 persons. The highest numbers were in some of the 3rd class conversions which seated 52 rather austerely, though this was exceeded in the 1932 electric thirds. Buffet and kitchen cars of course seated fewer passengers than parlour cars. There were minor variations from car to car, but seating of some "standard" cars can be quoted:

1908 "Southern Belle": brakes 30, parlours 33, buffet 25.
1910–2 SECR: buffets 19, parlours 24.
1921 12-wheel: parlours 36, kitchens 27.
1932 electric: 1st kitchens 20, 3rd parlours 56, motor 3rds 48, compos 12 1st, 16 3rd.
1951 "Golden Arrow": 1st parlours 26, 2nd parlours 42, 1st kitchen 22, 2nd brake 36.

The main change in styling over the years was in the windows. The first (1870s) Pullman design had seven sets of a narrow tall window with smaller ones each side, and two extra end windows. A little later, cars had seventeen small windows, and after that four square windows with smaller ones each side and two extra at ends. When cars began to be built in the UK, there were six large windows in the eight-wheelers and seven in the twelve-wheelers, though later the eight-wheelers also had seven windows. There were some exceptions to the above, specially in kitchen cars: some of the latter had one oval lavatory window between the main saloon windows and the kitchen portion, instead of at the ends. The acquired former SER "American Cars", and cars rebuilt from 1917 ambulance trains (see later) differed from the above styles.

The interior of the cars was quite unlike any ordinary carriages in terms of décor and use of materials. It would be tedious to go into the various styles; suffice it to say that the Victorian cars contained much sumptuous but stuffy furnishing, as one would have found in a wealthy drawing room; later a more Edwardian opulence was observable, and towards the end a perhaps healthy trend to simplicity. When new sets of cars were introduced the Press covered the décor rather more fully than the engineering. Much of the terminology is now obscure; for instance in the 1908 "Southern Belle" cars, four were recorded as being in "Adam" style, two in "Pergolese" and two in "French Renaissance" style. Descriptions were full of phrases like "damask silk" and "fine mohair velvet", and there is no doubt that such furnishings today would be out of the question.

Naming and Liveries

First class cars were always named until 1967; these names were used for identification in working time-tables. At first royal personages were used, followed by girls' names, precious stones and some romantic places. Some "courtesy" naming took place: Lord Bess-borough, Chairman of the LBSCR, Cosmo Bonsor, general manager of the SECR, and Lady Dalziel, wife of the Chairman of the 1908 Pullman Company, all had cars named after them.

When third-class cars came in 1915, they were not named, but had "Car No. X Third Class" on the sides. These "third class" numbers were not the same as the "schedule" numbers of the cars, which applied to cars of all classes existing in 1915 or later. In some cases, mostly late conversions or buildings, "third class" and "schedule" numbers were the same. From about 1948 the order of words was reversed; that is "Car No. 15 Third Class" became "Third Class Car No. 15"; however, from the end of 1949 cars as repainted were lettered only "Car No. X". From 1967 all cars only carried their schedule number; some had done so earlier for special reasons. For the boat trains on the SR and LNER some cars were rated "second class" but it seems that they were not painted "second class"; full details of second class usage are lacking. By the time third class became second class on BR, on 3rd June, 1956, it is doubtful whether any Pullmans still carried the old class on their sides.

The original livery was described as brown or mahogany. The word "Pullman" or "Pullman Restaurant (or other word) Car" appeared above the windows, with the name of the car in an oval cartouche below the windows. However, the LSWR cars had "Pullman Drawing Room Car" on their lower sides. From 1906 livery was entirely differ-ent: umber below window level, cream above. "Pullman" was in elongated gold lettering above the windows, and the name of the car in an ornamented frame of lining; there were coats of arms at each end of the sides. This new livery really only affected the LBSC: there is no photograph known to the author of an LSWR car in the new livery, and the SECR, when they began using Pullmans, had them painted in their own livery of dark lake and gold lining. On the Eastern Section of the SR cars in lake livery were still around as late as 1930. There was a slight change to the standard livery about 1930, the new umber being lighter and the cream darker, with the panels above the windows now umber and not cream.

From 1964 the official livery was changed to light grey with blue stripe along windows; no names were carried. However, few South-ern Region cars appeared in this livery; most were painted in BR colours, blue lower and grey upper, with the name of the train where the car's name had been, and the schedule number on the lower ends.

As detailed later, some cars were painted all-over green or umber for special reasons, and during the last War, while in store, in grey or red lead preservative paint.

Research into Pullman cars can sometimes be confused by the fact that certain names were used more than once; mostly this was a matter of late Eastern Region cars taking names of early SR cars; however, where there may be confusion the names are marked (I) or (II). Another possible cause of difficulty arose from the fact that in 1924/5 eleven cars were built in the UK and shipped to Italy for the use of the Compagnie Internationale des Wagon-Lits; they were named *Cynthia*, *Adrian*, *Ibis*, *Hermione*, *Lydia*, *Rainbow*, *Leona*, *Minerva*, *Niobe*, *Octavia*, *Plato*. All these, except *Hermione*, were returned to the UK in 1928, but only *Adrian*, *Ibis* and *Lydia* kept their names, the other names having been already re-allotted to other new cars.

As mentioned above, most cars not named after famous people carried names of girls or jewels; a few were named after places far away, such as Leghorn (Livorno); when a car was named *The Arundel* it was found that some passengers thought the car went there and the name was changed.

It can be a fascinating exercise taking any one Pullman car and pondering over its life experience; however, such a survey in print would take up too much space. One thing does seem to appear: that some cars saw a lot more excitement than others. Take the car *Lydia*; she was one of those built in 1925 and immediately shipped to Italy for the CIWL. Of the cars returned in 1928, she was one of the few to keep her name. She then spent some time on the LNER, but was on the "Bournemouth Belle" after the War; seen on the Special for President Tubman which did a noteworthy Southampton–Harwich run, also on Winston Churchill's funeral train; finally *Lydia* went to the USA in 1968 with the "Flying Scotsman" tour, and after travelling thousands of miles, remained there for preservation. She probably did a lot of other things too — reports of trains seldom gave the names of the Pullman; certainly there must be other cars which could show equally eventful lives.

No. 19544	No. 19544	
	The Pullman Car Company, Ltd.	
	PASSENGER'S CHECK	Good for this Trip only when accompanied by an appropriate Railway Ticket
Date...................	PASSENGERS ARE EARNESTLY REQUESTED TO SEE THAT TICKETS ARE TORN FROM A BOOK, CORRECTLY FILLED IN, SIGNED AND DATED, AND TO DESTROY THE TICKET AT THE END OF THE JOURNEY.	
	Car..One Seat	
	From........................to........................	
6/-	**6/-**	........................19........
HE. 740	SEE CONDITIONS AT BACK.	........................CONDUCTOR

Chapter Three
Early Pullmans on the LB & SCR

It was on 1st November, 1875 that the first Pullman ran from London (Victoria) to Brighton. This car, named *Mars*, had been obtained from the Midland Railway, having been assembled at Derby from imported parts. The speed of the train was not impressive, the journey taking 70 minutes, with six ordinary carriages attached. This car seems to have stayed on the LBSCR for some time, but was sent to Italy in 1883.

On 5th December, 1881 a complete train of Pullmans was put on, called the "Pullman Limited Express". Again the cars were ones assembled at Derby, a few years old: *Victoria* (ex MR *Adonis*), *Maud* (ex-MR *Ceres*), *Beatrice* (ex-MR *Globe*), and *Louise* (ex-MR *Ariel*); *Maud* was a smoking/luggage car. The train ran every day, but was not popular on Sundays and became weekdays-only for a time. When reinstated on Sundays it was called the "Pullman Drawing Room Train". A feature of this stock was that it was electrically lit from batteries charged by a steam engine at Victoria. The cars were finished in mahogany, with the name of the car in a cartouche on the side, and "Pullman Smoking Car" on the brake car above the windows. One account states that the other cars were lettered "Drawing Room", "Parlour" and "Buffet", but photos suggest they were all lettered "Restaurant Car". Two further cars assembled at Derby in 1877 are believed to have been on the line at this time. *Alexandra* and *Albert Edward*, though it is possible they did not arrive until the Midland Railway gave up Pullmans in 1888. *Jupiter*, which had been running on the London Chatham & Dover Railway from 1882, probably came to the LBSC in 1884.

On 11th December, 1888 a new three-car Pullman train began running to Brighton, comprising *Prince* (buffet), *Princess* (ladies) and *Albert Victor* (smoking). This set had side buffers at the outer ends only, the other couplings being of the type later known as "buck-eye". Lighting was supplied from a dynamo housed in a 6 w. LBSC van, painted in Pullman livery (No. 80). Another similar van was built in 1895 (No. 29); these became known as "Pullman Pups". Also in 1895 three new cars were supplied: *Her Majesty* (parlour), *Duchess of York* (buffet), *Princess of Wales* (smoking). From 1891 Pullmans were included in the Newhaven boat trains.

The livery at this time was described as "bronze, gold lines, roof rose, bogies dark brown picked out in yellow". Photos suggest that not all cars carried their names on the sides.

Ordinary carriages were attached to the Pullmans, though some trains were first-class only. There was to be no all-Pullman train until

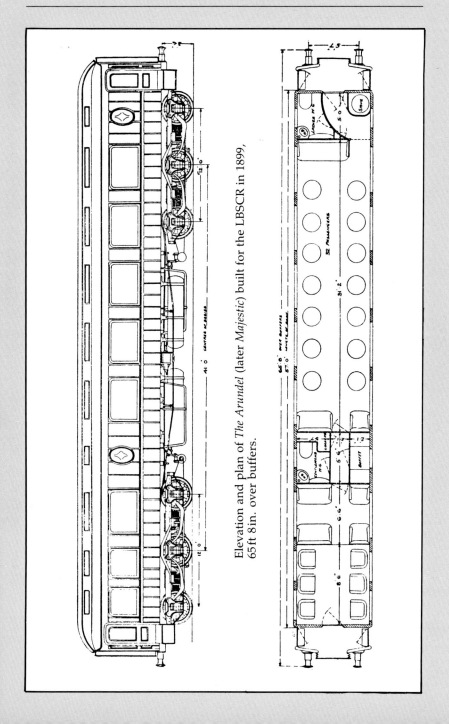

Elevation and plan of *The Arundel* (later *Majestic*) built for the LBSCR in 1899, 65ft 8in. over buffers.

1898, when a "Sunday Pullman Limited Express" was put on. The previous Sunday Pullman had run only in winter, as no path was available for it in the busy summer season, a problem which was to some extent solved by the opening in 1900 of the Redhill avoiding (or Quarry) line. The "Limited" made the journey in 60 minutes; however, most trains took 75 minutes or more, due to the practice of stopping for ticket collection at Preston Park (down) and Grosvenor Bridge (up); also most trains stopped at either East Croydon or Clapham Junction. The famous 5.00 pm from London Bridge (usually called the "City Limited") took 65 minutes, without ticket stop. The various Pullman trains available included the 9.25 am "Pullman Drawing Room Car Train" from Brighton, and "Pullman Limited" trains from Brighton at 1.20 pm and 5.45 pm. Timings and names varied from year to year. By 1898 there were 28 trains on the Brighton line including Pullman cars, the best taking just the hour.

Further Pullmans arrived from America: *The Queen* in 1890, *Pavilion*, *Princess May*, *Duchess of Connaught* and *Prince Regent* in 1893, *Duchess of York* and *Her Majesty* in 1895. In 1899 there was a change to six-wheeled bogies and longer bodies, with *The Arundel* (later *Majestic*), *The Chichester* (later *Waldemar*) followed in 1900 by *Devonshire*, and in 1906 by the last of the American-built cars, *Duchess of Norfolk*, *Princess Ena* and *Princess Patricia*. Meanwhile in 1899 the first Pullman write-off had occurred; *Maud* was virtually destroyed in an accident at Wivelsfield.

Pullmans were now running to Eastbourne, singly or in pairs; however, on Sundays there was a "Sunday Pullman", although ordinary carriages were also attached. From the summer of 1907 a new "City Limited" train was running, including three luxurious LBSC saloons vestibuled to a Pullman; one of the saloons had a brake portion housing a dynamo which supplied the whole four-car set; the rest of the train was of normal stock.

The presence of Pullmans in so many trains must have represented an extra burden on the locomotive power. For example, the 5 pm to London from Brighton had two portions, one for Victoria and one for London Bridge, and also took on some through carriages from Worthing. A typical formation noted for this train was: 5 bogies–Pullman– 3 bogies–bogie van (for Victoria), van–bogie–Pullman– 2 bogies (for London Bridge). It is not mentioned whether it was double-headed. In 1901 the London Bridge portion of this train was still being worked forward from East Croydon by a "Terrier" 0–6–0T; strange to think of a Pullman behind one of these tiny engines.

Speed as well as comfort was important on the Brighton run. On 26th July, 1903 a 5-car Pullman special behind the 4–4–0 *Holyrood* ran from Victoria to Brighton in 48¾ minutes, said to be the fastest-ever steam run. This compares with an officially-recorded 47 minutes in 1933 with two 6-PUL sets, and an unofficial 43 minutes on another run. It was no doubt with speed in mind that in 1907 Mr Marsh built his special 'I3' class 4–4–2T No. 21, with 6ft 9in. driving wheels; however, its performance does not seem to have been anything special, and no more "big-wheel" 'I3s' were built. Although tender engines were available, the LBSC always seemed to want the Brighton run to be regarded as a tank-engine job. The publicity for the new 1908 "Southern Belle" train showed the stock with an 'I2' class 4–4–2T at its head, though it seems doubtful whether this class could have kept time with a 280-ton load. The later 'J' 4–6–2T and 'L' 4–6–4T classes were tailored for this service and the latter class was still working when electrification came, though as loads grew ever heavier in SR days an infusion of "King Arthur" 4–6–0s was also necessary.

The year 1907 is a good one to leave the LBSC story for the moment: the 1908 "Belle" was the start of a new era, with the Pullman company under new management. Progress so far had not been impressive for Pullman; there were 27 cars running on the LBSC, but the Midland, Great Northern and Highland had given them up, the LSWR was phasing their few out, and the SECR was running its "American Cars" independent of Pullman at that time. Perhaps it was only a matter of time. Victorian England was very suspicious of foreign new-fangled ideas, and particularly the notion of sharing a carriage with a lot of other people, even though they be rich and well-behaved, did not appeal. It is interesting that in his book *The Railways of England* published in 1889, W.M. Acworth gives Pullman credit for introducing dining cars and bogie stock, but adds that he personally "would rather be boxed up in a Midland third class than have the privilege of enjoying the conversation of the public in the most luxurious car Pullman ever fashioned". The British loved their cramped compartment carriages; the openness of a Pullman took time to get used to.

Chapter Four

The South Eastern Response

The services to the short-crossing Channel ports must have seemed a natural opportunity for luxury travel ideas, and in 1874 the London Chatham & Dover Railway tried out two 6-wheeled sleeping cars of the Mann Patent Palace Car Co., a fore-runner of the Wagons-Lits company, but they were not a success. The next attempt was with a borrowed Pullman, *Jupiter*, which ran on the LCDR in a "Dover Pullman Car Boat Train" from 1st July, 1882 to 31st July, 1884, before being returned to the LBSCR. However, when the important Paris Exposition of 1889 came into view it was the Wagons-Lits company who jumped in, arranging with the LCDR for a luxury "Club Train" to run to Dover in connection with a new "Calais-Douvres" boat and new terminal at Calais. The train comprised three Belgian day-cars and a fourgon (a baggage/smoking/kitchen car), all painted green. Since the South Eastern Railway was required to pool its Continental receipts with the LCDR, it had to have a similar train; this consisted of two day-cars, a fourgon, and a six-wheeled SER brake-van painted green. From the French end, this seemed to be one train, leaving Paris at 3.30 pm and arriving at Victoria, Charing Cross and Holborn Viaduct at 11.15 pm. From the inclusion of the last-named, it seems that the LCDR train must have stopped at Herne Hill to shed one saloon. Neither company was happy with the financial results, and the trains were taken off on 1st October, 1893. The cars went back to Belgium, though the SER ones were noted as still in Rotherhithe Road sidings in 1895.

Although a semi-official history of the Pullman Company published many years ago refers to a contract having been signed with the LCDR in 1891, there is no record of any further cars on this line until after the LCD/SER fusion. The South Eastern Railway, however, seems to have felt there was a future for luxury trains; but there was to be a difference — the railway would own the cars. In 1891 they ordered from an American builder six cars of Pullman type: four "drawing room cars" (Nos. 32–5), one buffet car (No. 36) and a luggage car (No. 47), soon converted into another saloon. A special train of these cars was run for the press on 2nd March, 1892 from Charing Cross to Hastings. They had open platforms, but passengers could pass between them over footplates. They were now split up and run singly on various coast trains as first class saloons, no supplement being charged. In 1896 the cars were rebuilt with closed ends; Nos. 32–4 were converted to third class, and No. 36 was second class with an all-class buffet; they were formed into a train with six-wheeled vans Nos. 283/5, one at each end, all resplendent in lake red, gold-lined, and run as "The Hastings Car Train" from 1st December, 1896. This remained in service for many years; about 1905 the vans were replaced by 3-compartment bogie brakes, at least one of which (No. 2304) was second class.

In 1897 a further eight cars were purchased, from a British builder;

L.B. & S.C. Rly. The "Brighton Ltd."

Knight Series No. 1611.

The "Brighton Pullman Limited" about 1903, made up from the 1888 and 1895 Pullman sets with their respective "Pup" vans; van No. 29 leading.

Author's Collection

One of the early LBSC American-built cars at Newhaven Harbour about 1905.

Lens of Sutton

Duchess of Fife at Bournemouth about 1900 while working on the LSWR: this car later ran on the LBSCR. The looped line is an outside alarm signal.

Author's Collection

Duchess of Norfolk, a twelve-wheeled kitchen car of 1906, one of the last built in the USA; here seen working on the West Worthing service. *Lens of Sutton*

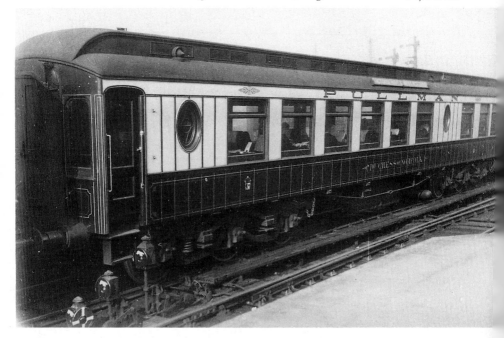

One of the cars built by the Gilbert Car Co. of the USA for the South Eastern Railway in 1891, later the Pullman *Dolphin*. *Author's Collection*

CHARING CROSS STATION. FOLKESTONE EXPRESS.

This postcard of about 1905 shows the Folkestone American Car Train at Charing Cross; note the odd roof line of the baggage car, with clerestory only over the saloon portion. *Author's Collection*

A down Continental special near Chislehurst about 1910, with three "American Cars", one "Gilbert" and two built by Metropolitan in the UK in 1897; all later sold to Pullman. *H.G. Tidey*

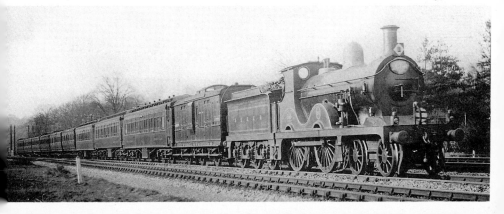

The "Southern Belle" on 20th September, 1923 with three of the 1908 cars leading. *O.J. Morris*

A Sunday all-Pullman Brighton train about 1924 with one of the third class parlour brakes rebuilt from an L & YR ambulance car leading; the locomotive is 'I3' class 4–4–2T No. 80. *Lens of Sutton*

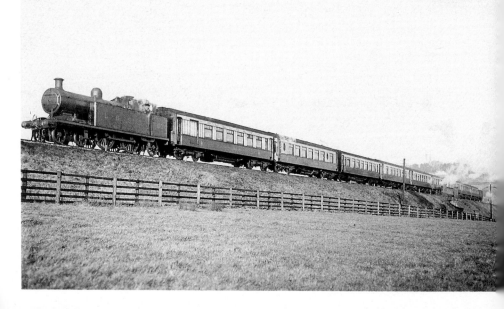

The "new" "Southern Belle" put into service on 1st January, 1925, photographed four days later at Quarry Box. *O.J. Morris*

A down Eastbourne train near Lewes on 17th July, 1934, with two twelve-wheeled Pullmans, probably *Myrtle* and a 1908 car. *O.J. Morris*

Rosemary, a parlour car built by Midland Railway Carriage & Wagon Co. for the LNER, as new in June 1923; this car later worked on the SR.

A race special on the Tattenham Corner line about 1924; 1910 cars topping and tailing a rake of converted SER "American Cars" all in red lake livery.

Lens of Sutton

The "Southern Belle" near Coulsdon about 1929, with three American cars in the formation.

R.W. Airy

The first "Bournemouth Belle" leaving Waterloo on 5th July, 1931; the leading cars are third class Nos. 40 and 84. *H.G. Tidey*

A Pullman Race Special approaching Epsom Downs station about 1932. *Lens of Sutton*

first class Nos. 201/2, second class No. 203, third class Nos. 204–6, third brakes Nos. 207/8. One car (No. 171) was also obtained from America. The eight cars formed "The Folkestone Car Train" which began running in 1897. No. 171 was apparently used for a time on a "Tunbridge Wells Car Train", and later with two of the other cars, a "Bexhill Car Train". The new stock differed from the earlier batch in having brake cars at each end with the clerestory roof over the saloon portion only, and a "birdcage" end look-out. In 1914 all fifteen cars were withdrawn and stored at Blackheath and other places, finally being sold to the Pullman Company in 1919; they returned with little alteration except to the brake coaches, as "Pullmans" with names as follows:

SER No.	Built	Type	Name	SER No.	Built	Type	Name
32	1891	B	Carmen	201	1897	B	Hilda
33	"	B	Constance	202	"	P	Dora
34	"	B	Diana	203	"	P	Mabel
35	"	P	Dolphin	204	"	P	Stella
36	"	P	Falcon	205	"	P	Dorothy
47	"	B	Figaro	206	"	P	Venus
171	1897	P	Tulip	207	"	B	Thistle
				208	"	B	Albatross

B – buffet; P – parlour

Chapter Five

Pullmans on the LSWR

This part of the story is brief; in 1880 the London & South Western Railway borrowed from the LBSC the Pullman car *Alexandra*, and worked it on the Exeter trains, but without much success. However, in 1888 the LSW was seeking ways to popularise the resort of Bournemouth, following the completion of its direct route via Sway, and after various improvements to the service, from 21st April, 1890 a Pullman was added to the 12.30 pm down and corresponding train up. Two cars were obtained, *Duchess of Albany* and *Duchess of Fife*, later joined (1893) by *Princess Margaret* and *Duchess of Connaught*. They were employed singly, and the other stock was not vestibuled in the early years.

In 1906 the LSWR decided upon a policy of using vestibuled trains with dining cars on its best trains; the diners were, however, to be built and owned by themselves, and the Pullmans were progressively set aside from that time. There is some doubt about when the last one ran; some sources place it as late as 1912. However, all did in fact pass to LBSCR service and at least one was there by 1907.

No Pullmans ran again on LSWR lines, apart from occasional specials, until 1931.

Chapter Six

Progress on the LBSCR and SECR

A new all-Pullman train entitled the "Southern Belle", which began running on 1st November, 1908 between Victoria and Brighton, broke new ground in many ways. It was the first train, except an earlier Sundays-only one, to make the journey regularly in 60 minutes. The seven cars were all twelve-wheelers, British-built, and the first not to have clerestory roofs; being 13 ft 2 in. high, they provided more head-room inside than before or since. Also for the first time food was actually cooked on the train, using a Fletcher-Russell gas cooker (later fitted in most other kitchen cars); up to now, previously-cooked food had merely been kept hot. The train was in the new umber and cream livery, and comprised end-cars *Verona* and *Alberta,* kitchen car *Grosvenor,* and parlour cars *Belgravia, Cleopatra, Bessborough* and *Princess Helen.* Each car weighed 40 tons, making a heavy train, but the tare weight per passenger did not work out too badly; the brake cars seated 31, kitchen 25, and parlours 33, total 219. However, an empty run each day was somewhat wasteful; the 5 pm up ran back to Brighton without passengers to form an extra 9 pm up. Also in 1908 an allegedly all-Pullman train to Eastbourne was put on, but it seems at times to have had ordinary carriages attached.

An even greater change was signalled on 12th September, 1915 when the LBSC began including third class Pullmans in two Brighton and one Eastbourne train. The cars were old "firsts" altered from a lounge-like layout to normal two-by-two seating; the supplement was only 9d. (4p). There is some confusion over the dates of conversions of cars, which carried no name but had "Car No. X Third Class" on the sides. The *Locomotive Magazine* refers to the "building" of cars 1, 3 and 4 in 1915, in fact converted from the old *Jupiter, Alexandra* and *Albert Edward.* All books so far published also refer to cars 17–19 being converted in the same year, from the *Duchess of York, Prince Regent* and *Princess of Wales,* but it seems odd that these numbers should have been given at that time, ahead of the post-War 11–16 series. Nos. 5–8 were twelve-wheelers built at Longhedge in 1917 (though this seems an odd thing to be done in the worst part of the War). Nos. 11–16 were 1921 conversions of LNWR ambulance cars; Nos. 9 and 10 were further conversions (*The Queen* and *Her Majesty*), various dates between 1917 and 1922 being given.

The omission of car No. 2 from the article in the *Locomotive Magazine* is interesting, for Mr F. Burtt stated that this was converted in 1895 from *Victoria*, though there is no record of third class at that time. Some of the number anomalies might be explained by the apparent existence at one time of a separate second class list; Nos. 17–19 for instance might have been second class cars, added to the third class list after No. 16 was built. Second class tickets were of course issued on the boat trains on the SECR, LBSC and Great Eastern, to fit in with second class on the vessels and the other side, but the extent to which Pullmans were provided so marked is not clear.

The early years of World War I were to some extent "business as usual" on the railways, but by 1917 it was biting hard, and all Pullmans, apart from three firsts and five thirds on the LBSC, were withdrawn. Some were restored on 1st October, 1919, but the "Belle" did not return until 1st October, 1921, running twice daily as a two-class train on weekdays, and on Sundays split into a first class and a third class train, both all-Pullman, the latter being referred to as the "Pullman Limited".

Meanwhile a contract had been signed with the South Eastern & Chatham management for Pullman cars to supplement their own American cars. Six were supplied, all first class: buffet cars *Corunna*, *Savona*, *Sorrento*; parlour cars *Valencia*, *Florence*, *Clementina*. They were run in parlour-buffet pairs, though the press was first treated to an all-Pullman run in April 1910. They were not finished in normal Pullman livery, but in the standard SECR dark lake with plenty of gold lining. They were eight-wheeled and weighed 9 tons less than the LBSC "Belle" cars, probably just as well in view of the gradients and locomotive power available. A further car, *Shamrock*, was supplied in 1911 for the Queenborough boat train, but this was transferred to the Caledonian later. In 1912/13 seven more cars came, *Alicante, Cosmo Bonsor, Mimosa, Ruby, Daphne, Topaz* and *Hawthorne*. This enabled Pullmans to be placed on more express trains to the coast, both on the Victoria–Margate–Ramsgate Harbour service, and Charing Cross–Folkestone–Dover–Deal.

The last arrivals before the War were four cars from a batch of twelve-wheelers intended for the Caledonian Railway. These Scottish-named cars, *Glencoe, Scotia, Hibernia* and *Orpheus*, are stated to have been placed at the disposal of the War Office for "top brass" visiting the Front. The first and last were not actually noted on the SR after the War and may have spent a few years elsewhere.

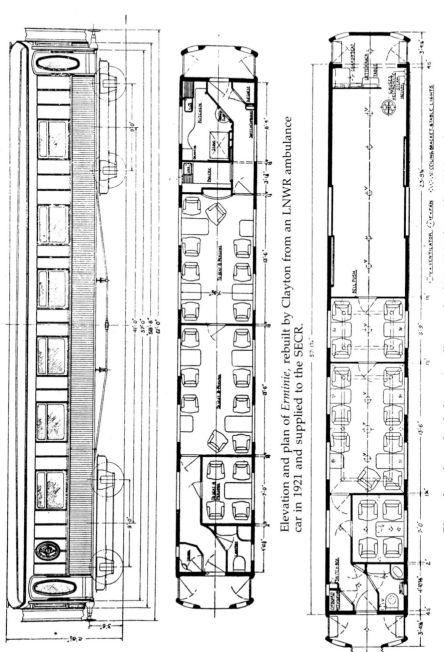

Elevation and plan of *Erminie*, rebuilt by Clayton from an LNWR ambulance car in 1921 and supplied to the SECR.

Plan of twelve-wheeled car *Arcadia*, as rebuilt in 1924 from the 1920 parlour car, with 23ft 8in. guard and luggage space; in 1934 became Third Class No.

At the 1920 Pullman Company Annual General Meeting, Sir David Dalziel stated that "the returns are only limited by the seats available", and "wider development would only be restricted by the amount of rolling stock they could place at the disposal of the railways". It was certainly a difficult situation. The company had signed up to provide a number of cars for the Great Eastern Railway, and the enginering industry, being still tooled up mainly for munitions, was not in the best position to build new cars rapidly. Sir David was either lucky or skilful; he was able to take over the fifteen "American Cars" of the SECR, which with minimal work were made into Pullmans; he also obtained twenty-two ambulance carriages from the LNWR, L&YR and GWR. All the railways had been asked to make up ambulance trains for moving war wounded to various hospitals, and in most cases the interiors had been so altered that there was no great eagerness to put them back to their original state. It is not certain how much of each vehicle was used but, even if they had to be stripped down to the frames, it was quicker than building completely new cars. In the event, new cars were built for the Great Eastern, the old SER cars were done up a bit for the SECR — though they had less than ten years' life in them, it was worth while — and the former ambulances, rebuilt during 1921, went out to the LBSCR except for six to the SECR and two to the Caledonian. Of twelve cars from the LNWR, six were rebuilt as first class (*Maid of Kent (I)*, *Anaconda*, *Erminie*, *Coral*, *Elmira* and *Formosa*), going to the SECR. All were rebuilt as composites in 1933. The other six became third class 11–16 on the LBSC; the L&Y cars (five) became third class 22–26, and three GWR ones, Nos. 20, 21 and 30, all on the LBSC. Two GWR frames became first class cars on the Caledonian.

There was some attempt to conceal the fact that second-hand vehicles were being used. The description of the ex-LNWR cars in *The Locomotive* in 1921 refers to their being "built" by Clayton. It says that the use of steel frames (hitherto most cars had been of integral build) was to save weight, and four-wheeled bogies were used for the same reason. It does appear that the bodies were probably all new; however, there was concern over riding qualities; extra rubber springs were fitted above the axle-boxes and rubber cushions placed between the frames and the bodies. The cars for the LBSC were finished in normal Pullman livery, but those destined for the SECR were in lake livery.

Some new cars were also being built, twelve-wheelers again for the SECR: *Padua* and *Portia* in 1920, *Calais*, *Milan*, *Palmyra* and *Rosalind* in 1921, and *Sylvia*, *Sunbeam*, *Malaga*, *Monaco*, and *Neptune* in 1922. These presented somewhat of a contrast with the converted "American Cars", some of which were forty years old, and the weight difference required close attention when making up trains so that permitted tare weight was not exceeded. The old cars soon came off the prestigious Continental runs; one was noted in 1929 still on a main line train, but they were mostly used on specials, the dark lake livery faded to a somewhat curious colour.

The Flushing Boat Train was revived for a short time, until this steamer service was moved to Harwich; it was reported as a short train, three coaches and one Pullman, usually *Regina*. It could be lifted up the steep Folkestone Harbour branch by two 'R' class tank engines, whereas some other trains required five.

The increasing supply of Pullman cars on the SECR enabled them to be put on trains to East Kent; a "Sunday Thanet Pullman" to Ramsgate began running on 10th July, 1921; this was later a mixed train, which came off finally in 1931. Some of the former SER "American Cars" were back on the Hastings line by 1922; published figures give the width of both batches of cars as 8 ft 4 in., but this may be an error in respect of the Hastings Car Train, as the Pullmans later built for this service were restricted to 8 ft 1 in., owing to a tight curving tunnel which put this line beyond Tunbridge Wells out of bound for most Pullmans.

From 1921 all services to the Continent except the Flushing service were switched from Charing Cross to Victoria; the area shared by Platforms 1 and 2, on the extreme east side of the station (where in fact the Pullman offices were), became noteworthy for the colourful departure scenes as Pullmans were boarded by top society; it was also later to be the short walk for royalties and notables of all countries between their Pullman Special and the Buckingham Palace landaus waiting in the yard.

It would appear from researches by Mr David Gould that in the early twenties the SECR had eight trains available for boat train duties. This railway had adopted a policy of having more or less permanently fixed trains; these were given as (for boat trains): Train No. 1, five twelve-wheeled Pullmans with first/second brake at each end; No. 2, six coaches, two Pullmans; No. 3, four coaches, three Pullmans; No. 4, four coaches, two twelve-wheeled Pullmans; No. 5, five coaches, two Pullmans; No. 6, four coaches, two Pullmans; No. 7, three coaches, two Pullmans; No. 8, two coaches, one Pullman. Trains Nos. 1 and 2 were all-gangwayed, others had some gangwayed carriages. However, the exigencies of service caused much second-rate stock to appear on boat trains, even after the construction of new stock set in hand by the SECR had been completed in 1924. It may seem remarkable that the SECR could allot nineteen Pullmans to the boat trains, find sixteen for Epsom Races, and still cover all other commitments. However, according to *The Locomotive*, at the end of

1923 there were 56 Pullmans working on the SECR against 54 on the LBSCR; there were only 34 on all other railways. It is ironical that the railway, thought by the public to have the worst rolling stock in the country, should also have more of the best than any other.

Chapter Seven
The Southern Railway 1923–39

Although the new Southern Railway followed the LSWR in most things, it did not follow it in turning its back on Pullmans. The use of these cars was extended on the SECR and LBSCR and brought back to the LSWR main line after an absence of twenty years. Somewhat oddly, the livery was not at first standardised, so that some Pullmans remained in lake livery on the Eastern Section until about 1930, and one or two in this livery strayed on to the Central Section. As stated at the end of the last chapter, the SR took over the working of a fleet of 110 cars. They were a mixed bunch; most of the ex-LBSC American-built cars were still running, so that clerestory roofs mingled with domed roofs even on the "Southern Belle"; the refurbished "American Cars" of the old SER were also running, with their clerestory roofs; there were also old and new twelve-wheelers, though no more were built after 1923.

Up to now there had been very little movement of cars between railways; the number series for third class LNER cars was started at 40, although the LBSC series ended at 36, and no car numbered over 36 was to stray on to the SR until 1931. With first class cars, there was no apparent demarcation — except that the Caledonian cars had very Scottish names — and no history of Pullmans has made clear in all cases what railway the cars were built for. An official photograph of four cars built in 1923 by Midland Carriage & Wagon has written on the back "built for the LNER", but two of them (*Iolanthe* and *Rosemary*) were noted on the SR in 1927. It therefore seems worth while to quote the list of Pullmans noted by the author running on the Southern Railway in 1927/8, even though it appears that a few were missed (listed at the end). It is perhaps difficult for readers of today to realise how long the idea of separate railways lasted into the grouping era; an ex-LBSC Pullman on the former SECR would have been a great event (though not very likely, as many were outside the SECR gauge). All the same, there must have been some interesting cases, which were not observed by the then small band of railway observers, for three of the massive "Hook Continental" twelve-wheelers

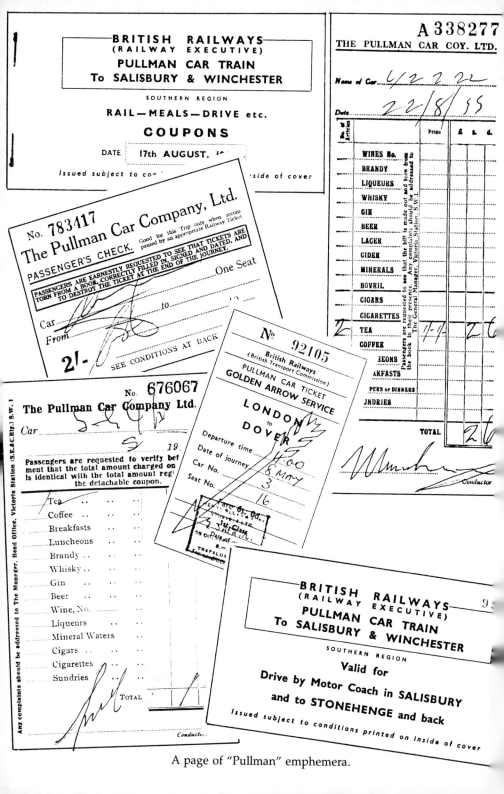

A page of "Pullman" emphemera.

PULLMAN
THE EMBODIMENT OF MODERN TRANSPORT

Imperial Airways
Empire Flying-Boat
PULLMAN
Car Train,
Waterloo to
Southampton,
connecting with
EMPIRE
AIR MAIL
SERVICES

**230
PULLMAN CARS**
are now in
operation
on the
Southern,
L.N.E.R. and
Metropolitan
Railways.

PULLMAN CAR COMPANY, LIMITED.
Victoria Station, London, S.W.1.

Telegraphic Address:
"Pullman, Rail, London."

Telephone:
Victoria 9978 (2 lines).

A 1938 Pullman Car Company Ltd advert.   *Courtesy: D.S. Lindsay*

A.B.C. Railway guide
can be consulted
on application to
the conductor.

Passengers are re-
quested to obtain
an official receipt
at time of payment.

THE PULLMAN CAR COMPANY LIMITED.

LUNCHEON 3/6

MENU

Mulligatawny Soup
or
Hors d'Œuvre

Choice of:-
Grilled Dover Sole
Roast Chicken & Ham
or
York Ham & Ox Tongue
Green Vegetables   Roast & Boiled Potatoes
Salad

Baked Apple Dumplings
Charlotte Russe

Cheese Celery Biscuits

C.   Coffee 4d.
No.4.

A 1930s Hastings Line weekday Luncheon Menu.   *Courtesy: D.S. Lindsay*

THE PULLMAN CAR COMPANY LIMITED.

21st Anniversary "Southern Belle"

November 1st, 1929

Luncheon 4s. 6d.

□

MENU

HORS D'ŒUVRE CHOISIS

CONSOMMÉ ROYALE

□

TURBOT POCHÉ   SAUCE HOLLANDAISE

□

CANARD RÔTI

CÔTELETTES D'AGNEAU REFORME

LEGUMES

BUFFET FROID

□

POUDING PRINCESSE

MACÉDOINE DE FRUITS AUX LIQUEURS

□

FROMAGE   CÉLÉRI   BISCUITS

□

CAFÉ

1929 Menu.   *Courtesy: D.S. Lindsay*

THE PULLMAN CAR COMPANY LIMITED.

November 21st, 1934

ROYAL SPECIAL TRAIN

Dover Marine to Victoria

⁜

LUNCHEON

MENU

⁜

CRÈME D'ASPERGES

⁜

TRUITE AU CHABLIS
ŒUFS COMTESSE

⁜

FAISON RÔTI
CÉLERI AU JUS POMMES PAILLES

⁜

SOUFFLÉ AU CHOCOLAT

⁜

DESSERT

⁜

CAFÉ

1934 Menu.   *Courtesy: D.S. Lindsay*

THE PULLMAN CAR COMPANY LIMITED.

CARTE DES VINS   DÉJEUNER

Aperitif Ricarlo
Xeres Sec   Hors d'Oeuvre Sainte Alliance

Chateau Yquem 1945   Filets de Sole Zena

                                 Selle d'Agneau du Southdown
Chateau Haut Brion 1945   Petits Pois du Lincolnshire
                                 Pommes Nouvelles Persillées

                                 Une Selection de Fromages
                                 Biscuits   Cœurs de Celeri

Martell's Cognac Liqueur   Parfait aux Trois Couleurs
Bols Kummel
La Invicta Petit Coronas

                                      Café Double

Mardi le 7 Mars 1950

1950 Menu.   *Courtesy: D.S. Lindsay*

of the former GER visited Longhedge Works in 1924 for rebuilding. Did they take the direct route via Shadwell and Peckham Rye, or some other? It is strange that record in the magazines of non-revenue movement of Pullmans is almost non-existent. All the cars in the following table were noted working in trains, and not in sidings or workshops, which explains why they are not quite complete.

TABLE ONE — PULLMANS NOTED RUNNING ON THE SR IN 1927/8

A: on Eastern Section. B: on Central Section. K: with Kitchen or Buffet. P: Parlour car. Bk: with luggage or guard section. L: running in red lake livery. X: scrapped before 1948. 12: twelve-wheeled.

(See end for names of cars not noted but believed to have been running.)

Albatross (1897) A K X L
Albert Victor (1888) B P X
Alberta (1908) B Bk 12 X
Alicante (1912) A K
Anaconda (1921) A K
Argus (1924) A K
Aurelia (1924) A K
Aurora (1923) A Bk L

Barbara (1926) A K L
Belgravia (1908) B K 12 X

Cadiz (1921) A P 12
Calais (1921) A P 12
Camilla (1926) A K
Carmen (1896) A K X L
Cassandra (1926) A K
Cecilia (1927) A K
Chloria (1928) A K
Clementina (1910) A K L
Constance (1896) A K X L
Coral (1921) A K X L
Corunna (1910) A K L
Cosmo Bonsor (1912) A K L
Cynthia (1925) A K

Daphne (1914) B K L
Devonshire (1900) B P 12 X
Diana (1891) B P X
Dolphin (1891) A P X L
Dora (1897) B P X L
Dorothy (1897) B P X L
Duchess of Connaught (1893) B P X
Duchess of Fife (1890) B P X
Duchess of Norfolk (1906) B K 12 X

Elmira (1921) A K L
Emerald (1910) A K L
Erminie (1921) A K L

Falcon (1891) A P X L
Figaro (1896) B P X L
Fingall (1924) A K
Flora (1923) A P Bk L
Florence (1910) A K L
Formosa (1921) A K L

Geraldine (1924) A K
Grosvenor (1908) B K 12

Hawthorn (1914) A K L
Hibernia (1914) A K 12 L
Hilda (1897) A K L X

Iolanthe (1923) B K

Juno (1923) A P Bk L

Latona (1926) A K
Leghorn (1910) A P L
Leona (1928) A P

Mabel (1896) A P X L
Madeline (1926) A K
Maid of Kent (1921) A K L
Majestic (1899) B P 12 X
Malaga (1921) A K 12 L
Marjorie (1924) A K
Medusa (1924) A K
Mimosa (1914) A K L
Monaco (1921) A K 12
Montana (1923) A P Bk

Neptune (1921) A K 12 L
Niobe (1927) A P

Octavia (1927) B K

Padua (1920) A P 12 L
Palermo (1910) B P
Palmyra (1921) A K 12 L
Pauline (1924) A K
Pavilion (1893) B P X
Plato (1927) A K
Pomona (1926) A K
Portia (1920) A K 12 L
Prince (1888) B P X
Princess Ena (1906) B K 12 X
Princess Margaret (1890) B P X

Rainbow I (1927) B K X
Regina (1910) A K L
Rosalind (1921) A K 12
Rosemary (1923) A P
Ruby (1914) A K L

Sapphire (1910) A P L
Sappho (1924) A K
Savona (1910) A P L
Scotia (1914) A P 12 L
Seville (1912) B K
Sorrento (1910) A P
Stella (1896) A P X L
Sunbeam (1921) A P 12
Sylvia (1921) A P 12

Theodora (1926) A K
Thistle (1897) A K X L
Topaz (1914) A P L
Tulip (1897) A P X L

Valencia (1910) A K
Venus (1897) A P X L
Verona (1908) B P Bk 12 X
Viking (1924) B K
Vivienne (1911) B P 12 X

Waldemar (1897) B P 12 X

Zenobia (1928) A K

CARS BELIEVED TO HAVE BEEN ON SR LINES AT THE TIME BUT NOT NOTED

Adrian (1928) K (3)
Bessborough (1908) P 12 (1)
Cleopatra (1908) P 12 (1)
Duke of Albany (1890) K (2)
Empress (1890) K (2)
Fortuna (1923) K (5)
Glencoe (1914) P 12 (5)
Ibis (1928) K (3)
Irene (1923) K (5)
Lydia (1928) K (3)

Milan (1921) K 12 (5)
Minerva (1927) P (4)
Myrtle (1911) K 12 (5)
Orpheus (1914) K 12 (5)
Pearl (1928) K (3)
Princess Helen (1908) 12 (5)
Princess Mary (1893) K (2)
Princess Patricia (1906) K 12 (2)
Stella (1921) P (2)

Notes: (1) 1908 "Belle" cars probably only being used on race trains.
       (2) Possibly stored as scrapped soon after.
       (3) Returned from Italy but not yet in service.
       (4) Probably on LNER at the time.
       (5) No explanation; just missed?

Only three cars on SR lines disappeared before 1927; *Mars* (1875) sold 1884; *Beatrice* (ex-MR *Globe* 1877) withdrawn 1918; *Maud* (ex-MR *Ceres* 1877) destroyed 1899.

1	ex-*Jupiter* (1875), 3rd from 1915.
2	ex-*Victoria* (1876), 3rd from 1918?
5–7	New in 1917, 12w.
9	ex-*The Queen* (1890), 3rd from 1920.
10	ex-*Her Majesty* (1895), 3rd from 1922.
11–16	rebuilt from LNWR ambulance cars 1921.
17	new in 1923, 12w., ex- No. 50.
20	rebuilt from GWR ambulance car 1922.
22–26	rebuilt from LYR ambulance cars 1922.
31–36	new in 1926.

All except 22/4/5/6 and 34–6 were kitchen cars; 25 and 26 were brake cars.

Regarding third-class cars not noted: No. 3 ex-*Alexandra* (1877) and No. 4 ex-*Albert Edward* (1877) may have been withdrawn. No. 8 was a rebuilt LNW ambulance car. No. 18 ex-*Prince Regent* (1893) and No. 21, a rebuilt GWR ambulance car, are said to have been working elsewhere as second class cars. Nos. 19 and 17 appear to be numbers left blank by the withdrawal of some old demoted first class cars, and filled by renumbering two Clayton twelve-wheelers on the LNER Scottish service, cars 51 and 50, to 19 and 17; 19 may not yet have been in service. With regard to Nos. 27–30, the information is not satisfactory. No. 27: sifting conflicting evidence, it seems likely it was built in 1923, then renumbered 80 (not on SR) and reverted to 27 when a new 80 was built in 1928. No information has been found on Nos. 28/9. No. 30 was a converted GWR ambulance car, possibly away at the time as a second class car.

EASTERN SECTION

In the early 'twenties "everyone who was anyone" had to take much of their pleasure in Paris, and they needed a luxury train to the short-sea-crossing ports. The Southern Railway was aware of this, but had inherited from the SE&CR little suitable stock; a train of old carriages with red Pullmans mixed in was not very grand. So the Pullman Company persuaded the SR to put on an all-Pullman train in the cream livery; this first ran on 17th November, 1924, and was usually referred to as the "White Pullman" or the "Dover Pullman Continental Express". In the season the train was made up to nine Pullmans, one first class brake, two six-wheeled flat wagons for the customs-sealed baggage boxes, and two vans. This totalled around 450 tons, depending which cars were used, and required double-heading until 1926, by when the bridges on the ex-SER main line had been strengthened to take a "Lord Nelson" or "King Arthur" 4–6–0. Then in 1926 Pullman got the Nord Railway of France to put on a similar train from Calais to Paris, and dubbed it the "Flèche d'Or" or "Golden Arrow"; under this name the Dover train also ran from 1929,

The down "Golden Arrow" passing Tonbridge on 26th April, 1947, decked out with the new motifs on engine and cars. *H.C. Casserley*

The rear of the "Devon Belle" at Exmouth Junction on 8th July, 1947; observation car No. 14, third brake 65, kitchen car 61. *H.C. Casserley*

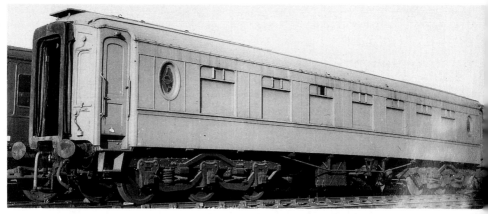

Calais in grey over-paint at Crystal Palace High Level station in 1946.

R.C. Riley

The former LNER car *Leona* rebuilt as third class No. 208 in 1947, seen here at Eardley Sidings.

R.C. Riley

The second *Maid of Kent*, the 1921 car *Formosa* renamed for the "Thanet Belle" in 1948.

Lens of Sutton

Rosamund, a 1924 car used in the post-war "Golden Arrow".   *Lens of Sutton*

Ibis, one of the 1924 cars sold to CIWL and returned in 1928, running on the Dart Valley Railway in May 1969; later on the VSOE Pullman train.

Lens of Sutton

One of the 1926 special restriction Hastings line cars, *Theodora*, as a "green Pullman" No. 184, working on the Southampton boat trains, at Clapham Junction on 29th February, 1960.   *H.C. Casserley*

The electric "Brighton Belle" on Battersea bridge in 1956; set 3051, Car No. 88, leading.   *Author*

The "New Century Bar" car, formerly *Diamond*, at Clapham Junction in July 1954, after being taken off the Ostend boat service, and before being renamed "Daffodil Bar" for the South Wales Pullman.   *H.C. Casserley*

The "Golden Arrow" leaving Victoria in 1956, hauled by "Britannia" class 4–6–2 No. 70014. The leading Pullmans are Car No. 35 and Car No. 34, 1926 cars as refurbished with square instead of oval lavatory windows.   *Author*

Ursula was one of the all-steel cars built for the "Queen of Scots" in 1928, here seen at Bournemouth in 1961.   *H.C. Casserley*

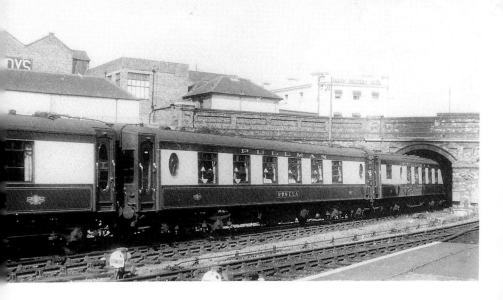

"Golden Arrow" stock leaving Victoria on 25th July, 1969 with the Pullmans in new liveries. *J. Scrace*

The "Brighton Belle" in new livery at Thornton Heath on 8th August, 1969. *J. Scrace*

The VSOE Pullman train visits Arundel on a special for Goodwood races, 11th September, 1982. *D. Gould*

The former "Brighton Belle" motor brakes of set 3053 stored by Allied Breweries at Manningtree, on 27th March, 1976; in 1977 they returned to Brighton as museum exhibits. *D. Gould*

The Pullman *Myrtle* crossing Canute Road, Southampton, on a boat train in May 1957. *H.C. Casserley*

Western Region DW150431 at Cardiff on 30th March, 1972, believed to be the former *Calais*, converted into a service vehicle after some years as a camping coach. *D. Gould*

The former "Brighton Belle" first kitchen car *Doris* as a firm's dining room at Finsbury Park on 26th March, 1977, after being repainted in its former livery at Derby. *D. Gould*

the 10.45 am from Victoria. From then the baggage cars mostly went down with the following 11 am, which took third class passengers but had four first class Pullmans. Both trains were often up to or over weight; for down trains the start was the hardest part and they were banked out towards Grosvenor Bridge by a 'T' class 0–6–0T puffing furiously. Often reliefs were also run, calling on the stock of red Pullmans.

The new Pullmans for this service were, firstly, four guard/parlour cars *Aurora, Flora, Juno* and *Montana*, the first three being outshopped in the old lake livery. Then there were kitchen cars *Argus, Geraldine, Marjorie, Sappho, Viking, Medusa, Pauline, Aurelia* and *Fingall*.

The "Golden Arrow" was all-Pullman until 1932, when some ordinary carriages were added. Its success declined in the "slump" years and at times it was reduced to four Pullmans. However, the Southern still regarded it as a prestige train and in 1938 provided refurbished coaches for it, in light olive green, to run with four "renovated" Pullmans. The re-launch of this train after the War is described later. After the strengthening of the SER line to Dover, the former LCDR line was dealt with, and relief "Continentals" often took this route. Some odd ones were seen, including a "King Arthur" with two Pullmans and a van — an easy trip for the fireman.

All-Pullman trains were run for VIPs, such as a visit from the King of the Belgians in 1936; one was occasionally also laid on for the P & O Lines as the first leg of a journey to Marseilles for a liner cruise starting there.

In 1924, following completion of the unscrambling of the SER/LCD competitive lines in the Margate and Ramsgate areas, a new service of London–Margate–Broadstairs–Ramsgate expresses was put on — sometimes called the Granville Expresses after some early special trains run for the Granville Hotel at Ramsgate. For this eight sets of new carriages were built, containing some fitted with adaptors for mating with Pullmans, and each set contained one first class Pullman car. At the same time a train was put on from Victoria to Dover via Maidstone East which included a first class Pullman. In 1926 six new first class cars were delivered for the Hastings service (via Tonbridge) of the restricted width necessitated by tunnels. These were: *Camilla, Latona, Madeline, Pomona, Theodora,* and *Barbara*. They worked singly, and from about 1933 became composites. Other new cars which came to the Eastern Section in 1927/8 were: *Cassandra, Plato, Cecilia, Chloria, Zenobia, Niobe* and *Leona*. They were needed, as the six former "Hastings Car Train" cars had to be withdrawn at this time; one (*Carmen*) had in fact been destroyed in the 1927 Sevenoaks smash when a "River" class 2–6–4T rolled off the track. The eight former "Folkestone Car Train" cars went in 1930: they had been on excursion work and never bore the umber and cream livery.

The multiplicity of alternative routes to the coast remaining from the SER/LCD rivalry meant that Pullmans appeared at times in some odd places, especially after the bridges on the LCD line had been strengthened. In 1937 the 2.55 pm from Ramsgate ran via Catford Bridge and actually stopped there, also at Lewisham, before taking the Nunhead Loop to Victoria. Two trains were running with Pullmans from Dover via Canterbury, allowing stations such as Shepherdswell to have a Pullman train stopping there. Cars were also appearing more and more on "foreign" excursions; one from Tunbridge Wells to Bourneville had a Pullman, and a Hastings line car was noted at Bolton on a football train.

In October 1936 the "Night Ferry" started running from Victoria to Paris and Brussels, most of the train crossing the Channel on new train-ferry vessels. Originally the formation was: five Wagons-Lits sleeping cars, three carriages, a Pullman and a van; however, the Pullman was soon taken off. The links between the Pullman Company and the Compagnie International des Wagons-Lits were too complex for full understanding; financial connections were well hidden, and it was customary in this country for Pullman people to deny any connection with CIWL. This confused many, as some cars on the other side of the Channel, undeniably CIWL property, also carried the words "Pullman Car".

This train, and the growing cross-channel air services, brought a steady decline in the number and loadings of Continental Expresses, and thus the number of Pullman cars on these trains, which for 25 years had seen the matching of "beautiful people" to "beautiful Pullmans" as nowhere else.

CENTRAL SECTION

The only event of note in the early years on the former LBSC line was the announcement that an "entirely new" "Southern Belle" train would run as from 1st January, 1925. The splendid 1908 train had only seen some 13 years of service, due to the War, but perhaps its weight and low seating capacity caused the decision to take it off. The Southern Railway often used the word "new" merely to mean "different" and this was certainly the case here. The third class cars were some of those rebuilt in 1921 from former ambulance cars; the first class cars, in so far as they can be traced, seem to have been some post-war ones originally intended for the LNER or the Eastern Section of the SR, including *Iolanthe*, *Viking* and *Rosamund*. Although the Section had two third class "end-cars" (Nos. 25/26) they do not seem to have been used, as photographs show the train with bogie brake vans at each end at first. The steam "Belle" had only another seven years to run, and during this period it was very variable in format: the Sunday first-class-only train had to lean heavily on the old American cars. With an electric "Belle" already a gleam in the eyes of certain parties at Waterloo, there was naturally no incentive to make much of the steam version. The 1908 twelve-wheelers were also used to help out — two of their 1911 look-alikes (*Myrtle* and *Vivienne*) were on the train in 1931, by which time there were seven thirds and only three firsts on the weekday train.

One prestige train which had not included a Pullman in recent years was the "City Limited", the 8.48 am from Brighton and 5 pm from London Bridge. In 1925 an entirely new train of Eastleigh-built stock was provided for this, but still no Pullman. However, in February 1926 one "first" was taken out and the car *Princess Patricia* put in. It is perhaps worth recording here that cars seldom stayed long on one stint; on this duty *Grosvenor* appeared later in 1926, followed at roughly yearly intervals by *Iolanthe, Regina, Anaconda* and *Coral.* Some regular travellers may have formed an affection for an individual car, but if they did so the Pullman Company did not respond. Perhaps only railwayists noted names; a correspondent in *The Railway Magazine* in 1954 recalled that the Pullman in the London Bridge portion of the 5 pm from Brighton fifty years earlier "was usually *Jupiter*" — so at least someone remembered them.

. In 1926 the new "King Arthur" class 4–6–0 was introduced to the Brighton fast trains, though the "Atlantics" and "Baltic Tanks" also continued on the rosters up to the last days. From contemporary records it seems that all were equally capable. In June 1931 an "Atlantic" took the "City Limited" down in 56½ minutes net; an "Arthur" with the same 400-ton load equalled this time from Victoria; and a 4–6–4T with 430 tons had a 58½ minutes net time in the up direction.

The electric "Southern Belle", which began running on 1st January, 1933, represented a brave move, but perhaps an unnecessary risk, for the quick turn-around that was the main advantage of multiple-units was not really necessary for this duty. The question was: could a 62-ton motored car, of which there was one at each end of the three five-car "Belle" sets, provide the sort of comfortable running that Pullman passengers expected? On the opening run, a group of madrigal ladies strolled along the train to show how quiet and smooth it was. In the opinion of the author, who was a passenger, the test failed — and they could only stroll half-way down each way as there was no connection between sets. However, these sets remained in use for forty years and achieved affection from regular travellers, who perhaps left the end cars to day-trippers. At a ceremony in Brighton on 29th June, 1934, the train was renamed "The Brighton Belle".

Incidentally, the original name was inspired by W.S. Forbes of the LBSC, nephew of the famous J.S. Forbes of the LCDR. The "Belle" sets were originally numbered 2051–3, and named cars were: (2051) *Hazel* and *Doris*, (2052) *Vera* and *Audrey*, (2053) *Mona* and *Gwen*. The third class cars as usual carried only numbers, 85–93.

Also on 1st January, 1933 six-coach EMUs took over the express working to Brighton. These sets included a composite Pullman in each. There were twenty 6-PUL sets (2001–20), and three 6-CIT sets (2041–3) with initially more first class accommodation as was required for the City Limited. After a short time one set was swapped for a West Worthing Pullman working, and the train ran as 6-PUL+6-CIT. For the first two years almost all Brighton expresses in peak hours had two Pullmans, though as there were no corridors through motor coaches, passengers could not make contact with each other. From 1935 when 17 more six-car sets were built for the Eastbourne and Hastings line, with pantry cars, it became customary for trains to be 6-PUL+6-PAN on both Brighton and Hastings lines.

The composite cars in the 6-PUL and 6-CIT sets all had names, as follows:

2001	*Anne*		2011	*Naomi*
2002	*Rita*		2012	*Bertha*
2003	*Grace*		2013	*Brenda*
2004	*Elinor*		2014	*Enid*
2005	*Ida*		2015	*Joyce*
2006	*Rose*		2016	*Iris*
2007	*Violet*		2017	*Ruth*
2008	*Lorna*		2018	*May*
2009	*Alice*		2019	*Peggy*
2010	*Daisy*		2020	*Clara*
2041	*Gwladys*	2042 *Olive*	2043	*Ethel*

Set numbers were altered to 3XXX in 1937.

After the Brighton electrification, work was found for the displaced Pullman cars partly on the Eastbourne and Bognor trains; after the former line was also electrified there were even more spare. However, business in Pullman Specials was good; not only race specials, but also royals and semi-royals, and trips to important business and State events. The 1935 Derby Day saw two all-Pullmans specials on the Epsom Downs line, both double-headed with two tank engines, and at least two more to Tattenham Corner in charge of 'N' class 2–6–0s. On occasion SR Pullmans were lent to the LNER for Newmarket race specials. As there were seldom any "end-cars" available for these specials, something had to be provided for the guard. The

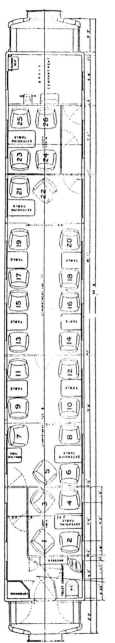

Plan of Brake Cars *Aurora, Flora, Juno* and *Montana*, Southern Railway (SE & C Section). Seating capacity 26 passengers

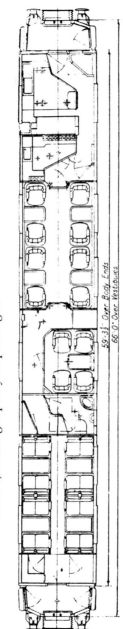

Plan of one of the composite cars used in the 6-PUL electric sets of 1932; 66 ft over vestibule plates.

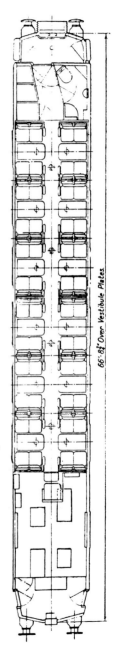

Plan of one of the motor brakes of the 1932 "Southern Belle"; 66 ft 8¾ in. between nose and vestibule plate.

Central Section had three unusual bogie brakes, two with clerestory roofs (928/9) and one of "Balloon" outline (909) and these were most often used, perhaps because they gave a better impression than the flat-roofed varieties.

Despite all this, however, Pullmans were being scrapped, and in some cases the bodies sold for as little as £50. One such on Bishopstone beach had noble company, an equerries' saloon from the LBSC royal train and a "first" from the old City Limited. In the period 1929–32 forty-eight cars were taken out of service on the SR, including all but two of the pre-1908 ones, and all the converted SER American cars. Official figures early in 1933 gave the Pullman Co. as having 112 first class cars, 40 composites, 73 thirds, and 32 dining cars (mostly on the LMS). As all the cars on the LMS would be sold to that railway in 1933, it is clear that the peak figure for Pullmans in traffic must have been passed some time during 1932, the actual date depending on the inter-action of withdrawals with the commissioning of new electric cars. The number schedule begun in 1915, including all cars in service at that date and later, had reached 300 by 1933; only one non-SR car had been withdrawn.

In 1935 the Pullman Company took a hard look at its future requirements on the Southern Railway. The fleet was now reasonably modern; almost all the American cars went in a sweep in 1932, and the few left then were now gone. There were the old 1908 "Belle" cars, heavy twelve-wheelers. Mr. G.H. Griffith, general manager, announced "no further use is in prospect for them". So they all went except one, *Grosvenor*, which was converted into a bar car, as was *Myrtle*, one of the 1911 twelve-wheelers. Although earlier Pullmans had had small "bars", the new conception was for a long bar with seats, and a few more at the end of the car. It was for passengers to move in and out of; both cars were seen on the Newhaven boat trains and were popular. A few old cars were painted all-over umber and put on to cheap excursion trains, but details of their use are scarce. The Bognor and Portsmouth line was of course still finding employment for Pullmans, but electrification was in progress and was completed by 1938. The new trains were to have restaurant or pantry cars, not Pullmans; by 3rd July, 1938 there were no Pullmans in regular steam-hauled service anywhere on the Central Section.

However, the Pullman Co. could congratulate itself on one score. The King and Queen had made little use of the Southern Railway Royal Train of late, and in fact in 1939 it was demoted to work the Brookwood Necropolis service. For some years Pullmans had been used instead, and the frequent press photographs of royal personages stepping from Pullman cars at Platform 2 at Victoria helped to keep up the Pullman image. The Company never had an official

"Royal Saloon" though no doubt care was taken in choosing the stock, which usually ran to four cars, to accommodate the entourage. For example, when Their Majesties paid a state visit to France in July 1938, *Minerva* was used; on their return from their Canadian tour in June 1939, *Niobe* was the Royal Saloon.

WESTERN SECTION

Pullman cars returned to the former LSWR in January 1931, when some cars were put on the Ocean Liner Expresses to Southampton, usually two to four per train. These were mainly cars which had just had a very short term with the Great Western Railway: *Evadne, Loraine, Ione, Joan, Juana, Eunice,* and *Zena*; also six former "Queen of Scots" cars.

On 5th July, 1931 came the inaugural journey of the "Bournemouth Belle", serving Bournemouth and for a time Weymouth. The train was summer-only on weekdays from 1931 to 1936, though it ran on Sundays in winter. After the first summer season, the Weymouth portion was discontinued. This had comprised five coaches from the ten-car train, taken off at Central before the remainder went on to Bournemouth West. As usual, it was announced as an entirely new train, but in fact only four cars were new. The formation was: third class cars 40, 84, 82, 60, first class *Flora, Montana, Aurelia,* third class 81, 83, 41. Only cars 81–4 were new, the rest being of 1920–5 build. The handsome end-cars, Nos. 40/41, had originally been built for the Great Eastern Railway in 1920, but only four years later were rebuilt as brakes for the Great Northern section of the LNER. The brake and luggage compartments measured 22 ft. Two first class cars, *Ansonia* and *Arcadia*, with the same history, which later came to the SR as thirds 94/5, had 23 ft 8 in. luggage spaces. These long brake-ends, painted brown all over, made a break from tradition on the SR. The rolling doors were fitted during the 1924 rebuild.

The early stirrings of long-distance air transport also brought work for Pullmans in this area; special trains, usually of four cars, were run as required to Bournemouth for Hurn Airport, and Poole for the flying boats. The latter also worked for a time from Hythe (Hants), the Empire Flying Boat Service, and passengers were ferried across Southampton Water using Hythe Pier, to and from a single Pullman and van, joined up with a boat train within the Docks.

Under the dynamic control of the Southern Railway, Southampton increased its traffic enormously, and Ocean Liner Expresses and Pullman Specials proliferated. An observer in 1932 noted 17 up Ocean Liner Expresses one day, 12 with Pullmans. Pullmans were also included in the Channel Islands boat trains, and on 15th August, 1936 one of them, *Rainbow,* caught fire *en route* and had to be detached while burning at Micheldever. This was especially embarrassing since the following train was the "Bournemouth Belle" loaded to twelve cars. Such a load could not be taken round the steeply-graded Alton line to avoid the fire, so it was run-round at Winchester, worked tender-first to Eastleigh, sent to Salisbury where it reversed, and arrived at Waterloo three hours late. No doubt the drinks profits for the day were high.

TABLE TWO — DOWN PULLMAN TRAINS IN THE 1931 WINTER TIMETABLE (WEEKDAYS)

Central Section

		Class of Pullman
8.50 am	Victoria–Portsmouth	3rd
9.05	Victoria–Brighton	1st & 3rd
10.00	Victoria–Newhaven	1st (two)
10.05	Victoria–Brighton	1st & 3rd
11.05	Victoria–Brighton	1st & 3rd. All Pullman
11.15	Victoria–Eastbourne	1st & 3rd
12.05 pm	Victoria–Brighton	1st & 3rd
12.35	Victoria–Brighton SO	1st & 3rd
1.00	London Bridge–Brighton SO	1st & 3rd
1.10	Victoria–Brighton SO	1st & 3rd
1.48	London Bridge–Eastbourne SO	1st
2.05	Victoria–Brighton	1st & 3rd
3.05	Victoria–Brighton	1st & 3rd. All Pullman
3.15	Victoria–Eastbourne	1st & 3rd
3.20	Victoria–Bognor	1st & 3rd
3.35	Victoria–Brighton	1st & 3rd
3.35	Victoria–W. Worthing	3rd
4.00	London Bridge–Brighton	3rd
4.05	London Bridge–Eastbourne	1st
4.35	Victoria–Brighton	1st & 3rd
5.00	London Bridge–Brighton SX	1st
5.05	London Bridge–Eastbourne SX	1st
5.08	London Bridge–W. Worthing SX	1st
5.20	Victoria–Eastbourne	1st & 3rd
5.35	Victoria–Brighton	1st & 3rd
5.40	Victoria–W. Worthing	1st & 3rd
6.00	London Bridge–Brighton	3rd
6.05	Victoria–Brighton SX	1st & 3rd
7.05	Victoria–Brighton	1st & 3rd
8.05	Victoria–Brighton	1st & 3rd
8.20	Victoria–Newhaven	1st (two)
10.05	Victoria–Brighton	1st & 3rd
11.05	Victoria–Brighton	1st & 3rd
12.05 am	Victoria–Brighton	1st & 3rd

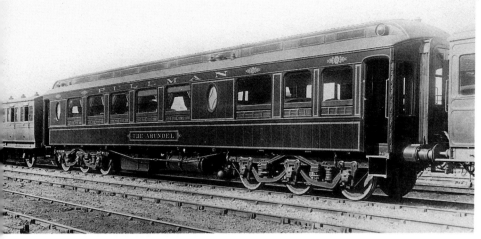

The Arundel, an 1899 twelve-wheeler, which was renamed *Majestic* in 1905.
R.C. Riley Collection

Duchess of Fife, one of the 1890 LSWR cars which later worked on the LBSCR, here seen at Gatwick in 1934 some time after withdrawal. *R.C. Riley Collection*

Albatross began life as SER No. 208 in the Folkestone Car Train. From 1919 to 1931 it worked as a first class Pullman car, then spent eight years as a supply car at Preston Park, and finally became, as here, a mobile office at Lancing Carriage Works. *R.C. Riley Collection*

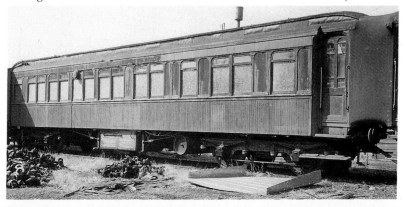

Grosvenor, the kitchen car in the 1908 "Southern Belle", which was rebuilt as a bar car in 1936.   *R.C. Riley Collection*

Isle of Thanet, renamed from the 1928 *Princess Elizabeth*, to work on the "Thanet Belle".   *R.C. Riley Collection*

Prince was originally the centre car of the LBSCR 1888 3-car set; seen here about 1920 at Longhedge.   *National Railway Museum*

The scene at Preston Park depot after the bombing of 25 May 1943; third class Car No. 20 right, No. 40 on its side, and No. 12 destroyed.
R.C. Riley Collection

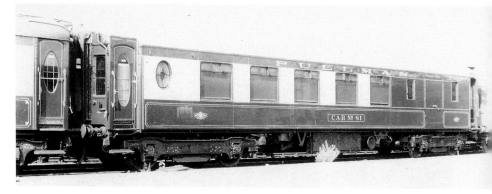

Brake car No. 81 Third Class was built in 1931 for the "Bournemouth Belle"; here it shows off the new 1959 coat of arms.   *Lens of Sutton*

Neptune, originally a lake-liveried 1921 kitchen car, at Longhedge shortly before withdrawal in 1960 to become an Eastern Region camping coach.
Lens of Sutton

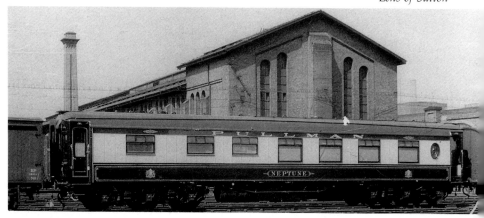

Former Third Class Car No. 15 as camping coach P41 about 1963.
Lens of Sutton

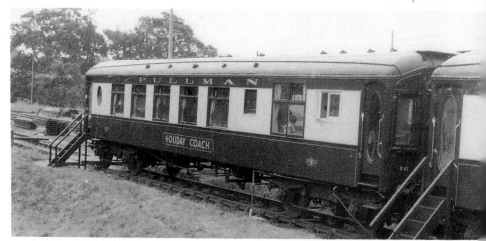

Plato, a 1926 kitchen car. *Lens of Sutton*

Car No. 54 had a varied life: built in 1923 for the LNER, later on SR, retired to Tyseley Museum 1960, and then in 1980 sold to Sea Containers for the VSOE, finally to the Bluebell Railway in 1986. *Lens of Sutton*

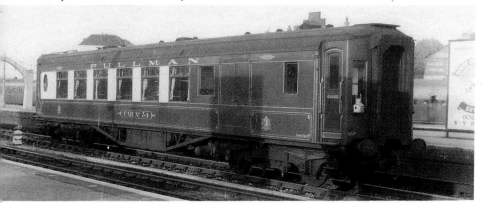

Ruby ran in the SECR lake livery from 1914 to 1930; later it spent some time on the Le Havre Boat Train. The original bogies have been replaced. *Lens of Sutton*

The 1910 car *Emerald* as instruction car No. 101 about 1960.   *Lens of Sutton*

The 1908 "Southern Belle" car *Grosvenor* was rebuilt as a bar car in 1936.
Lens of Sutton

Third class kitchen car No. 17 was formerly (briefly) No. 50, built in 1923.
Lens of Sutton

Originally a conversion from an LNWR ambulance coach, Car No. 11 was rebuilt as a brake car in 1946.
Lens of Sutton

Pegasus, built for the 1951 "Golden Arrow", was equipped with the Trianon Bar.   *Lens of Sutton*

Juno was one of the 1923 cars for the "White Pullman"; seen here about 1948.
                                                                                    Lens of Sutton

Eastern Section

Former SER main line: 1st class Pullman:

11.30 am	Ramsgate SO	All from Charing Cross except 5.00 pm, from Cannon Street.
12.55 pm	Margate SO	
1.15	Ramsgate SX	
4.15	Ramsgate	
5.0	Ramsgate	
5.15	Ramsgate SO	
7.15	Margate	

Former LC&D main line to Ramsgate: first class Pullman on following trains from Victoria: 8.55 am, 10.34 (SO), 11.25 (SO), 1.10 pm (SO), 3.10 (SO), 3.15 (SX), 6.08 (SX), 7.00, 9.00. From Cannon Street, 1.12 pm (SO), 5.06 (SX), 5.16 (SO), 5.46 (SX), 6.08 (SX).

Hastings line: 1st class Pullman, from Charing Cross: on 10.40 am, 12.25 pm, 3.20, 7.20; from Cannon Street, 1.04 pm (SO), 5.04, 6.00.

Continental trains, all from Victoria: Folkestone–Boulogne, 9.00 am, 10.00, 2 pm; Dover–Calais, 11.00 am (all-Pullman), 11.15, 4.00 pm. Ostend served by 10.00 am and 2.00 pm. All trains advertised as 1st or 1st/2nd only, except 4.00 pm which served 3rd class for destinations outside France. It does not appear that any Pullmans other than 1st class were used.

Western Section

9.00 pm	Waterloo–Southampton–Havre	Timetable implies a Pullman.

It is worth while looking also at the Sunday service on the Brighton main line, as this was a field-day for Pullmans, especially 3rd class ones. The "Southern Belle" was first-class-only all day, and ran down at 11.05 am, with two return trains from Brighton at 5.00 pm and 7.05. The "Pullman Limited" which was all-Pullman and third class only, went down at 9.45 am and returned from Brighton at 6.35 pm. In addition there was an all-Pullman two-class train, not named, which left Victoria at 11.35 am and returned from Brighton at 4.35 pm. The "Eastbourne Sunday Pullman", 1st and 3rd, left Victoria at 10.45 am and left Eastbourne (not all-Pullman) at 6.20 pm. With four all-Pullman trains leaving Victoria in under two hours in winter-time, the popularity of the cars could not be doubted — however, it must have called for some shunting on Saturday. It must be remembered that there were also two boat trains with Pullmans each way, and other trains to Worthing, Brighton and Eastbourne with the usual quota of two cars. The morning train to Portsmouth which included only a third class Pullman also ran on Sundays, but via Dorking instead of via Crawley and took the opportunity of stopping at Dorking North, surely the only Pullman train to serve this station.

Chapter Eight

Southern Railway — The War and After

In September 1939 all Pullmans were locked or withdrawn in the first panic of War. The "Bournemouth Belle" suffered the indignity of being pushed into Tolworth goods sidings. However, on 1st January, 1940 new orders took effect and some were restored; *The Railway Magazine* reported that by May 1940 there were 36 Pullmans working on the Central Section and 24 on the Eastern; after the fall of France the pattern changed and in May 1941 there were 48 on the Central and 22 on the Eastern. One "Brighton Belle" set was running usually attached to a 6-PUL set; however, after set 3052 had been heavily damaged by bombs near Victoria on 9th October, 1940, all the three sets were withdrawn. On 22nd May, 1942 all Pullmans were finally withdrawn, except those on War service, and the 6-PUL sets became five-coach.

Some cars were made use of; one case was the special train which ran each night from the north-west end of Victoria station, near the then BOAC terminal building, to Bournemouth for Hurn airfield and Poole for the flying boats. The passengers were mostly in the VIP category; when noted in 1945 the train comprised only two Pullmans, a first class carriage and a van.

Some major damage was done when on 25th May, 1943 bombs dropped on the Pullman train-shed at Preston Park. Third class cars 12, 20 and 40 were destroyed and others damaged; another bomb on Brighton a month later damaged a further nine cars.

While the War was on not much notice was taken of the former Pullmans now running in various guises. From 1942 some were on hire to NAAFI and had their own number series; a few seem to have been semi-static. As the War ended ten NAAFI cars were allocated to five BOAR leave trains; these were still running as single cars into 1947. All seem to have been green, although some brown cars were also seen on other jobs. One person who did take some notes in 1944, Mr R.C. Riley, has kindly allowed these to be used here; of course they only take in a proportion of the Pullmans either in use or stored at conveniently quiet locations.

Crystal Palace High Level, 22nd January, 1944: "Belle" set 3052 tarpaulin-covered, badly shrapnel-pitted.
Horsted Keynes, 28th February, 1944: *Sylvia, Cadiz, Sunbeam, Padua.*
Polegate, April 1944: *Topaz, Glencoe, Aurora.*
Eardley Road Sidings, 17th May, 1944: in original livery, *Pearl, Sylvia, Grosvenor, Myrtle*; in khaki, *Sappho, Monaco, Anaconda.*
Aldershot, 19th May, 1944: Car No. 19, grey (seen next month at Eardley).

Burgess Hill, 24th June, 1944: *Mimosa, Hawthorn, Florence, Madeline,* two more.

Coulsdon North, 24th June, 1944: nine cars from 6-PUL sets: *Olive, May, Bertha, Brenda, Rose, Grace, Enid, Gwladys, Daisy.*

Preston Park, March-June 1944: *Fingall,* Car 24, *Leona, Clara, Iris, Aurora, Aurelia, Myrtle, Grosvenor.*

Tonbridge, August 1944: *Savona.*

Sidley, August 1944: Car 31, *Malaga, Neptune, Orpheus, Hibernia.*

Polegate, October 1944; *Eunice, Evadne, Zena, Juana, Lucille, Loraine, Ursula, Leona.*

Cars were certainly moving around, though probably mainly for painting and preserving; no cars had been varnished since the beginning of the War, and those that showed signs of deterioration were treated with red or grey lead oxide paint.

When the War ended a lot of movement began; the LNER cars had been stored on the SR, and cars of both railways did not all return whence they came, some SR cars going on to the "Queen of Scots" and "Tyne-Tees", and some LNER cars on to the "Golden Arrow", and so on. The electric cars, when dragged out of store, did not all return to their original sets.

Thoughts of re-starting Pullman services were quick to arise; as early as October 1945 a ten-car all-Pullman train was noted behind "Merchant Navy" Pacific No. 21C2 on a proving trip to Dover, and the same train was seen early in 1946 behind electric locomotive No. CC2 doing a twice-daily run to Brighton, not in public service. One of the "Belle" sets was working from 24th April, 1946, coupled either to a 4-COR or 6-PUL set; however, repairs on the bomb-damaged set 3052 were now being done and the train was fully restored on 6th October, 1947. Pullmans were replaced in the 6-PUL sets as from early May 1946.

On the Hastings (former SECR) line Pullmans were also restored, but only three cars, and these were de-classed and lost their names, simply carrying "Restaurant Car" on the sides. No supplement was charged. The three cars were *Barbara, Madeline* and *Pomona*; their schedule numbers (182, 183, 185) were also carried on the sides. The other three former Hastings line cars were transferred to work on Southampton Boat Trains.

In view of the enormous difficulty in procuring any supplies such as paint or timber, the Pullman Company did very well to restore services — and start new ones — as soon as this did. There were few observers with the opportunity to cover developments as they unfolded; however, Mr R.C. Riley was again able to take some interesting notes (all 1946):

> 13th September, cars 32 and 33 noted newly painted in Brighton carriage sidings (these were later on the "Devon Belle").
>
> 28th September, in South Croydon sidings (the old terminal station platforms): *Scotia* (brown), *Topaz*, Car No. 11, *Aurelia*, Car. No. 8 (grey), Car No. 13 (green), Car No. 30, *Leghorn*, *Elmira*, *Erminie*.
>
> 30th September, at Stewarts Lane: Car No. 1 (the second, ex-*Emerald*) green livery.
>
> October, in Lancing Works: *Grosvenor*, *Myrtle*, *Camilla*, *Vera*, *Ruby*, *Padua*, *Ibis*, *Latona*, *Fingall* (later on the "Tyne-Tees").
>
> 25th October, at Preston Park: *Myrtle* with roof cut down to allow working over Eastern Section (this was one of the 13 ft high cars).
>
> 27th December, Preston Park: *Cynthia*, *Vera*, *Regina*, *Loraine* (brown), *Eunice*, *Lucille*. At Burgess Hill: *Formosa*, *Malaga*. At Hove: Car No. 9, *Palmyra*.

The work of overcoming wartime depredations and complications went on; a visit to Preston Park on 14th February, 1947 revealed, amongst others, *Zena* in green livery, *Princess Elizabeth* in red lead, and Car No. 26 as LNER 489.

The "Golden Arrow" was restored from 15th April, 1946. There had been a run for the press on the 13th, rather marred by the fact that the new "Trianon Bar" Car, former 3rd class car No. 5 entirely rebuilt, ran hot on the way down and had to be taken off; the other cars were *Lady Dalziel* (bk), *Adrian*, *Sappho*, *Niobe*, *Onyx*, *Cecilia*, and 2nd class cars 194 (ex-36) and 154 (ex-*Flora*, bk.). The former car *Diamond* was hastily got up as a "Trianon Bar" for the 15th, but No. 5 returned in July and served until 1951 when the new "Arrow" stock appeared. (*Diamond* was possibly the only car to serve on all four Regions of BR; she was renamed "One Hundred Bar" and then "New Century Bar" for the Ostend boat trains, then having a centenary, and in 1955 "Daffodil Bar" for the WR South Wales Pullman, later going on to both Eastern and London Midland under various guises.) The new "Golden Arrow" was decked out with gold arrows and "Golden Arrow" and "Flèche D'Or" on both engine and Pullmans.

The "Bournemouth Belle" was restored on 7th October, 1946. It was considered that its future lay mainly with third class passengers, and it only had four first class Pullmans (*Philomel*, *Ibis*, *Rosemary* and *Lydia*); the third class cars were 17, 19 and 94–99; these last were six former first class cars, two from the LNER. This made a twelve-car train, but at slack times two or four cars were taken out.

A new all-Pullman train began running on 20th June, 1947, the "Devon Belle", from Waterloo to Ilfracombe, with initially a Plymouth portion dropped at Exeter. This ran on summer weekends, Friday to Monday, and from 1948, Tuesdays and Thursdays also. The two trains providing the service both had observation cars, made out of old third class cars, which required turning and running round at termini; another unusual feature was that for the first few years the train did not stop at Salisbury, engines being changed at Wilton. As this train spent most of its life under BR, it will be dealt with in the next chapter.

In post-war conditions more third class cars would be needed; some were created instantly by screwing number boards over names. Demotions included four of the six cars rebuilt in 1921 from LNWR ambulances; *Anaconda, Erminie, Elmira,* and *Maid of Kent* (I) became third class Nos. 132, 133, 135, 137. There were no numbers 134 or 136, because *Coral,* which would have had the first number, was not demoted, and *Formosa,* which would have been 136, was renamed *Maid of Kent* (II) for the "Thanet Belle". There was also a call for more "end cars" and several were so rebuilt at Preston Park.

This was a time when many Pullman-watchers became confused over numbering. Although the original "third class" series retained its low numbers, new conversions to third class took their higher "schedule" numbers, though illogically when cars 11, 15 and 16 were converted to brakes they kept their old numbers, as did 13 and 14 when made into observation cars. The highest numbers in the old third class series were 105–7 for some "Yorkshire Pullman" cars in 1946. Those quoted above, 132/3/5/7, were *schedule* numbers used as third class numbers. A good example of how confusion could arise is provided by cars 94–99. Nos. 94/5 (ex-*Ansonia* and *Arcadia*) did not take their schedule numbers, which were 108/9, when converted to third class: however, cars 96–99 *did* take their schedule numbers. Schedule 94 and 95 (*Neptune* and *Sunbeam*) stayed first class.

Chapter Nine

Under British Railways

It might have been expected that the private Pullman Car company would be ground into British Transport Commission anonymity after nationalisation, but this was not so. In fact in many ways this was to be the period of the most use of Pullmans. In 1948, however, the fact had to be faced that no new cars had been built for sixteen years; it was fortunate that few of the cars made redundant by the electrification programme had in fact been scrapped. One of the first new Pullman trains, the Sunday "Eastbourne Pullman Limited" needed

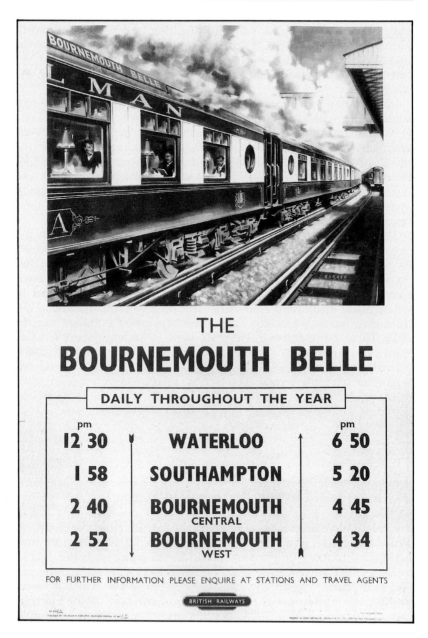

A Railway Executive Poster advertising the "Bournemouth Belle".
Courtesy: D.S. Lindsay

none since it used a spare "Brighton Belle" set. This first ran on 31st May, 1948, and on the same day the "Thanet Belle" (later renamed "Kentish Belle") was put on between Victoria and Ramsgate. This had eight third class cars and only two first class. It was made up from old cars — but there was no shame in that. The present Queen's honeymoon train used the Pullmans *Rosemary* and *Rosamund*, so twenty-year-old cars were adequate for her. As with a woman, one did not ask a Pullman car her age.

The launching of the "Devon Belle" has been mentioned in the last chapter. There were two trains of twelve cars each, and each was tailed by an observation car. These cars, Nos. 13 and 14, were former third class parlour cars, rebuilds from LNWR ambulance carriages. In their new form they had built-in bars, and 27 seats facing a sloping glazed end. A correspondent in the Press commented that these were made uncomfortable enough to deter any one passenger from staying too long. Fortunately, the excellent view of an 'N' class 2–6–0 banking the train up to Mortehoe summit was of interest only to railwayists — otherwise there would have been a mad scramble somewhere around Braunton. The front four cars in both directions were the Plymouth section, detached at Exeter. The formation just before nationalisation had been: Plymouth portion, Cars 54, 33, *Argus*, Car 208; main train, *Princess Elizabeth, Rosamund, Geraldine*, Cars 34, 249, 32, 27, 13. Second train, Plymouth portion: Cars 55, 61, *Iolanthe*, Car 36; main train, *Minerva, Cynthia, Fingall*, Cars 35, 169, 60, 63, 14. A year later eight of these had changed; in summer 1948 the formations were: Train No. 1, Plymouth portion: Car 36, *Iolanthe*, Car 54; main train, *Princess Elizabeth, Ibis*, Cars 34, 33, 32, 27, 13. Train No. 2, Plymouth portion, Car 208, *Cynthia*, Car 55; main train, *Minerva, Penelope*, Cars 35, 61, 31, 65, 14.

This train was not a great success; from 1950 on the Plymouth portion was dropped, and in 1952 it was announced the train would not run; however, it was reprieved as a week-end only train until September 1954. By that time it was bearing witness to the continuing demoting of first class cars, since it included third class cars 161 (ex-*Fortuna*), 162 (ex-*Irene*), 166 (ex-*Geraldine*), 167 (ex-*Viking*), 171 (ex-*Pauline*), and 248 (ex-*Lady Dalziel*). Ilfracombe did in fact see one more Pullman train when, on 19th October, 1963, the *Flying Scotsman* arrived there with a Pullman Special.

During the week, and after the train's demise, the observation cars were in demand for special trains; from the operational point of view, it was better if these were round tours and called for no observation car turning. When in April 1951 part of the "Devon Belle" was used for a visit to the Grain oil terminal, the whole train was turned on a triangle inside the complex; there were other triangles such as those at Branksome and Eastleigh which could come in useful. As related later, the two cars finally went to Scotland, but one is now back in Devon still rolling happily after seventy years in various guises.

It was the preparations for the 1951 Festival of Britain which gave Pullman car construction a much-needed boost. It was considered that the influx of tourists for the event would justify new Pullman trains, which would also serve for the very many VIP specials expected. An order placed with Birmingham C & W in 1938, which had not been progressed, was restarted with some modifications to design, and the following new cars appeared in 1951: first class: parlour cars *Perseus*, *Cyanus* and *Hercules*, bar car *Pegasus*, kitchen cars *Aquila*, *Orion* and *Carina*: also second class car No. 303. Most of these were put on to a new "Golden Arrow". In addition, the 1927 first brake *Minerva* and second brake car 208 (formerly LNER *Leona*) were refurbished, as were former third class cars 34–6 of 1926; in 1952 two more new cars came from the Pullman works, *Phoenix* (on the frame of burnt *Rainbow*) and *Aries*. The new "Golden Arrow" first ran on 11th June, 1951, the formation being: *Minerva*, *Aquila*, *Cygnus*, *Pegasus*, *Hercules*, *Orion*, *Perseus*, *Carina*, second class Car No. 35, second class Car No. 208. *Pegasus* contained a new "Trianon Bar". Not long after this the train lost its down end "end-car" and usually ran with a bogie utility van, or a four-wheel van plus baggage car; later still with a GUV at each end.

The new cars, which were built on LNER-type frames with 8 ft 6 in. double-bolster bogies, differed only from the old style in having square, instead of oval, small windows. They were used on many VIP specials, usually four-car, and perhaps the smartest ever seen, with the "Merchant Navy" Pacific picked out in white on wheel rims and bosses, buffer faces, brake pipes, smoke deflector edges. Usually it carried an armorial device of the country concerned in a round panel over the smoke-box door.

For the 1951 season the "Thanet Belle" was renamed "Kentish Belle" and ran twice daily on weekdays, as it always had on Saturdays. During the "Festival" period a portion of the train was detached at Faversham and worked to Canterbury. Soon after, this "Belle" became a mixed train, and ceased to run on 14th September, 1958.

A development of 1952 was the naming of various Southampton Boat Trains, for instance "The Cunarder" and "The Statesman" (United States Lines), some workings being all-Pullman.

Motive power was of course changing; the "Bournemouth Belle" was first diesel-hauled in October 1951, though still mainly steam, including oddly enough in May 1953 the ex-LNER 'V2' Pacifics, at a time when "Merchant Navy" class engines were temporarily with-

R902

e SER Gilbert Car No. 32 used for
Hastings Line service. It
ame Pullman Car *Carmen* in
9, only to be destroyed in the
renoaks crash in 1927.

Photograph: D. Lindsay Collection

e all important section of the
lman Car – the cooking range –
n here in car *Argus* c.1957.

Photograph: D. Lindsay Collection

Two views of the beautiful marquetry details in the wall panels of the Pullman Car *Barbara*, now in use on the Kent and East Sussex Railway.

Photographs: D. Lindsay Collection

Attendant Hawkes (*left*) seen here showing off the new range of silver to the cook in the car *Perseus*. *Photograph: D. Lindsay Collection*

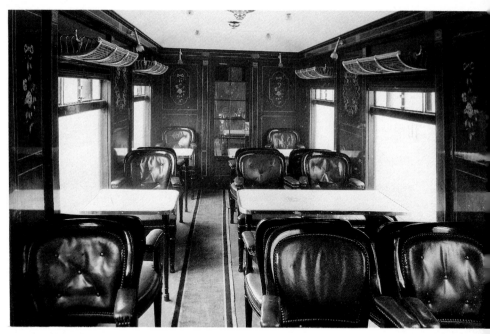

These two photographs show the comparison of *Barbara*. The top picture depicts the layout after the 1946 refit, whereas the lower is the scene after 1984.　*Photographs: (top) D. Lindsay Collection and (bottom) J. Berryman*

Following the opposite page is a comparison pair of photographs showing the Bar end of *Barbara* with the (*top*) 1946 refit containing a pink Formica counter top.   *Photographs: (top) D. Lindsay Collection and (bottom) J. Barryman*

The Bar area of Pullman Car *Diamond*, photographed at the time of the New Century Bar. It had previously been pressed into service as the Trianon Bar in 1946. *Photograph: D. Lindsay Collection*

The seating end of car No. 5, the original "Trianon Bar" for the "Golden Arrow", 1946. Note the aluminium plaque showing that London and Paris were connected by the "Golden Arrow". This plaque can now be seen at Beer Modelrama in Pullman car *Orion*. *Photograph: D. Lindsay Collection*

Interior of car *Malaga* after refurbishment for the Royal Train and "Golden Arrow" service (*c*.1950). This car is now preserved by Ian Allan Ltd at Shepperton.   *Photograph: D. Lindsay Collection*

An unusual interior of the car *Mimosa*, decorated in yellow with mirrored and marquetry panels.   *Photograph: D. Lindsay Collection*

The fine interior view of car *Sappho* of 1924 with its 22 seats.
Photograph: D. Lindsay Collection

Finally an interior view of a third class car, No. 303, built in 1951 for the "Golden Arrow" service. *Photograph: D. Lindsay Collection*

drawn. The easily-forgettable diesels 10201/2/3 were seen on the "Bournemouth Belle" and the "Golden Arrow", and electric loco 20001 on race specials to Epsom Downs. In 1953 all Pullman train headboards were re-designed, partly to make them easily transferable between engine classes; all had been designed to fit the Bulleid Pacific lamp-iron placings.

At the end of the last chapter the 1947 "Bournemouth Belle" was described. By the mid-fifties only four of those cars were still on it, Nos. 17 and 97–9; the first class cars were now *Topaz, Hibernia, Sunbeam,* and *Rosalind*; replacement thirds were Nos. 6, 47 and 303. This last car, a brake, was allotted its schedule number as its "third class" number when built in 1952 — though in fact it ran as second class No. 303 for a time on the "Golden Arrow". In 1960 some more Eastern Region cars, displaced by new stock, came to the SR; by the time the "Bournemouth Belle" died, on 9th July, 1967, three of them, *Ursula, Phyllis* and *Lucille* were on it, also *Aquila,* and seconds 34, 61, 64, 75, 76, all but one originally LNER. The twelve-wheeled end-cars had gone, and there was a van at each end.

In 1964 Lord Beaulieu took on to his museum site a "Schools" 4–4–0 and three Pullmans, exhibited as "The Bournemouth Belle"; the cars were *Fingall, Agatha,* and Car No. 35, though it is not certain that *Agatha,* a "Queen of Scots" car, had ever worked on the Southern. In 1972 the cars went to Haven Street, IoW, but later *Agatha* came back, for the VSOE (see later) and *Fingall* for the Bluebell Railway.

Now that much of the Pullman traffic was in Specials, they popped up in some strange places; in November 1954 a "Royal" for the Emperor of Ethiopia from Portsmouth to Victoria went via Mitcham Junction; one for the Queen ran to Fort Brockhurst. Even the "Brighton Belle" sets strayed; there were three recorded occasions when sets ran from Waterloo to Portsmouth on specials, one a "Royal" for the then Princess Elizabeth. Two Pullman trains appeared in London Docks in February 1954 when a strike diverted a liner from Southampton; the route from Waterloo was circuitous and no doubt the trains caused astonishment passing through Dudding Hill and Putney Bridge. Two other notable trains are worth a mention: a train of twelve first class Pullmans from Victoria to Erith for a works visit, and a Lourdes Pilgrim Train with Pullman kitchen cars interspersed with WD ambulance coaches.

Two other Pullman specials of 1953 were unusual; firstly they ran from Southampton to Victoria, and there was no easy route, there being no connection at Clapham Junction or via the West London Railway for the main line, and a rather sordid route via Wimbledon,

Tooting and Streatham Junction was usually chosen. Secondly, they were carrying passengers from the cruise liner *Caronia* to view the Coronation, and this involved the trains leaving the Docks about 4 am! In the mid-fifties, a rather attenuated Royal Train was noted on several occasions, comprising two "Restriction O" brake coaches each side of the Pullman *Aquila*; however the Royal race train to Tattenham Corner was always four-car.

The Region had now gone a long way towards fixed-interval trains on all services, and therefore the tally of Pullman services can be simply presented, for instance for the 1955/6 winter table:

> *Central Section:* Brighton Line: trains with Pullmans ran on the hour from Victoria from 9 am to midnight, the 11 am and 3 and 7 pm workings being the all-Pullman "Brighton Belle". Exceptions were the 5 pm City Limited which ran from London Bridge, as also a 6.05 pm which split at Haywards Heath, the Pullman-equipped portion going on to Brighton and that with a pantry car to Littlehampton. Littlehampton trains were at 25 minutes past, from 9.25 am to 7.25 pm; however, the 12.25 was SO and there was no 1.25 or 6.25. There was also a 10.45 pm shared with the Hastings line, splitting at Haywards Heath. Eastbourne and Hastings line; hourly at 45 minutes past from 8.45 am to 10.45 pm, but the 1.45 was SO; also a midnight train shared with Brighton. The 9.05 am boat train to Newhaven also included a Pullman.
>
> *Western Section:* 12.30 Waterloo to Bournemouth (all-Pullman). Also Southampton boat trains.
>
> *Eastern Section:* 11.35 am Victoria to Ramsgate was a supplement train, any composites working on other lines counted as refreshment cars only. The Dover continental train now ran at 10 am from Victoria, the Folkestone trains being at 12.30 and 1 pm, the latter being the "Golden Arrow" at this time running via Folkestone instead of Dover. The former carried Ostend passengers, who also had a 9 am with Pullmans.

In 1959 a new coat of arms was adopted by the company. Put in non-heraldic language, the only difference seemed to be that the lions supporting the shield were horizontal rather than vertical. The company was now in the throes of a face-lift which had been agreed in 1955, namely the introduction of multiple-unit diesel Pullman trains, intended for businessmen's routes. The new trains, in six-car sets for the London Midland Region and eight-car for the Western, appeared in 1960, in a new blue livery, with a grey stripe, changed later to grey with a blue stripe. These trains were very rare visitors to the SR, but sets were noted at Salisbury on 25th April, 1970, at Brockenhurst on 25th March, 1971, and at Ashford on 21st July, 1972. In 1966 when the ex-LMS main line was electrified, the two "Manchester Pullman" trains were redundant, and they were offered to all the other

Regions. The Eastern seems to have said no after a trial, the Southern
without a trial, and they went to the Western.

The only redundancies amongst the traditional cars caused by the
above transfer were those in the South Wales Pullman, but neverthe-
less there were far too many loco-hauled Pullmans in traffic and in
1960 a wholesale conversion of cars to camping coaches was begun,
these being made available to all Regions. The SR was ultimately to
receive 25, the first going to Corfe Castle, Sandling and Wool. They
had bunks for six, kitchen and large lounge, and cost a little more to
hire than a normal carriage conversion. On the SR they kept their
Pullman livery, with "Holiday Coach" or "Pullman Camping Coach"
on the sides, with a 'P' number painted at the off-side end; other
Regions had different liveries and number systems. Some outlasted
the passenger service to the stations at which they were located,
causing some servicing problems. The numbers of the SR cars were:

No.	Formerly	No.	Formerly
P40	Car No. 11	P53	*Valencia*
P41	Car No. 15	P54	*Florence*
P42	Car No.16	P55	*Regina*
P43	*Coral*	P56	Car No. 8
P44	Car No. 30	P57	Car No. 6
P45	*Ruby*	P58	*Hawthorn*
P46	*Hibernia*	P59	*Padua*
P47	*Rosalind*	P60	*Daphne*
P48	*Sunbeam*	P61	*Leghorn*
P49	*Rainbow*	P62	*Sorrento*
P50	Car No. 47	P63	*Corunna*
P51	*Sapphire*	P64	*Palermo*
P52	Car No. 98		

These conversions were carried out over a period between 1960 and
early 1963.

Equally depressing was the fate meted out to the former Hastings
line cars. In 1958 these six, plus the *Hadrian Bar* (former Car No. 59),
were sold to British Rail (Southern Region) and painted green without
names, lettered "Buffet" and with the schedule numbers (180–185) on
the sides. In 1961 these were numbered into SR stock, S7872S to
S7877S in the following order: *Camilla, Latona, Theodora, Madeline,
Pomona, Barbara* (schedule numbers 180, 181, 184, 182, 183, 185). The
Hadrian Bar was numbered S7879S. They were used mainly on the
Southampton Boat Trains, the last of which with a Pullman ran in
June 1963; the "green Pullmans" were also all withdrawn by that
time.

On 11th June, 1961 the "Golden Arrow" was electric-hauled for the first time, the great conversion of the old SER main line being completed. This was also a time of many line closures, and some "last trains" featured Pullmans. There was one on the last train over the Kent & East Sussex Railway on 11th June, 1961 (though a few years later the new Tenterden Railway would own two Pullmans and trains would run again). The first and last all-Pullman train on the Somerset & Dorset Railway ran in December 1961 to Blandford Forum. The company also sensed the need to preserve something, and took *Topaz* (I) out of service to restore it to original 1914 form (though not livery) complete with a pair of 1913 bogies; it went for a time to the Clapham Transport Museum in London.

In the autumn of 1963 an extra run each way was put on for the "Brighton Belle"; the down run was at 11 pm and the stock was brought into Victoria at 10 pm for late dinners. However by this time the Pullman Company was really no more; in 1962 the BTC had purchased the remaining shares, and on 1st January, 1963 the BTC became British Railways Board, with Pullman being in effect a part of the British Transport Hotels & Catering. The "Belle" continued to be in the news; on 18th August, 1963 faster running was tried, and a trip done in 51½ minutes; but the verdict was that it was too rough for the public. Then on 28th March, 1964 Charter Trains Ltd began to charter the "Belle" at week-ends for "a night of gambling at Brighton". This did not last long; no doubt its presence in the small hours when the maintenance people felt they ought to have the line was an irritant — on occasion it was loco-hauled with ER Pullmans "owing to electric power not being available", and also diverted via Shoreham.

The 1928 LNER car *Joan*, which had been put at Winston Churchill's disposal during the War, and was later much used by General Eisenhower, had come to the SR in 1960, and when the General was visiting Britain in 1962, this car was sent up to the Midland Region for a sentimental (and press-covered) reunion.

From May 1965 the "Golden Arrow" became officially a mixed rather than all-Pullman train, a recognition in fact of a state of affairs which had occurred on occasion before this date.

What was probably the most-publicised Pullman train ever ran on 30th January, 1965 — the funeral train for Winston Churchill, which was on the SR from Waterloo as far as Reading. The cars used were *Carina, Lydia, Perseus,* and *Isle of Thanet,* the coffin being in bogie van No. S2464 painted in Pullman livery.

The same year saw the beginning of withdrawal of the 6-PUL sets from the former LBSC main lines, to be replaced by 4-COR units which had no Pullmans. The last 6-PUL ran on 24th April, 1966, and the Pullman presence on the Brighton line was now confined to the

"Belle". On 9th July, 1967 the "Bournemouth Belle" also went, and again the new electric stock did not include Pullmans.

There were still a few Pullmans in service on the Eastern Section boat trains: 306 *Orion*, 302 *Phoenix*, 301 *Perseus*, 305 *Aquila*, 307 *Carina*, 247 *Isle of Thanet*, and Car 208. As stated earlier, in 1964 the official Pullman livery had been changed to grey with a broad blue stripe covering the window area, but the Southern Region elected to paint most of their cars in BR livery, and the "Brighton Belle" appeared first in this livery in November 1968. The name of the train appeared where the old car names had been, and the schedule number at each end of the lower portion; first class cars had a large figure 1 on the doors. A similar treatment was applied to "Golden Arrow" cars. The Southern Region timetable still made passing reference to Pullmans, the London–Paris section having certain trains keyed as "first class accommodation is provided only in Pullman cars and second class only in ordinary carriages". However, the entries on the Brighton line table for the four "Belle" trips made no mention of Pullmans.

There were still nine trains on BR which were all-Pullman or nearly so, but eight would be taken off in the next ten years. The first to go was the "Brighton Belle", on 30th April, 1972, no doubt because it was the oldest stock by far. The next was the "Golden Arrow" on 30th September, 1972, because electric multiple units had proved more handy, and what passengers thought of the trains was no longer considered important. So although so-called Pullmans in various blue liveries would go on running for a few years on other parts of the railway system, for the Southern Region it was the end of the Pullman. However, they were certainly not going with a whimper. Tribute to the "Brighton Belle" began even before public service ended: a "Brighton Belle Commemoration Tour" was run on 1st April, 1972, in the course of which set 3053 ran from Waterloo to Victoria via Portsmouth, Eastbourne and Brighton.

In 1971/2 people suddenly woke up to the fact that Pullmans were either gone or going, and interest greatly increased. Notes in *The Railway Magazine* reveal this; on 24th August, 1971 Car No. 340 was seen on an excursion from the Western Region to Ramsgate, still in umber and cream livery. This was probably one of half a dozen transferred in May of that year from the East Coast to the Western Region for excursion work. In January 1972 a "Brighton Belle" set was once again seen at Waterloo on a Portsmouth excursion. Meanwhile the activities of the Bulmer's Cider Pullmans were eagerly followed. These were former third class cars 36, 64, 76 and 83, and first class *Aquila*; they were painted in a Pullman style livery, but the colours were green, white and red. They had been purchased in 1968 and later teamed up with the preserved engine *King George V* to run excursions from their Hereford base, including a widespread tour of the Western Region on 2nd–9th October, 1969.

Another focus of interest was Pegler's "Flying Scotsman USA" which covered thousands of miles in America from 1969 onwards, the train including the Pullmans *Lydia* and *Isle of Thanet*. The "Devon Belle" observation car No. 14 was also on the train. All were destined to be preserved, the first two at the National Railroad Museum at Wisconsin, and in fact *Lydia* was handed over to the USA Ambassador by Prince Philip at a ceremony at Kensington (Olympia) station. Unfortunately bankruptcy halted the train in 1972.

The last day of the "Brighton Belle", 30th April, 1972, was "celebrated" in style. There had been enormous objection to the ending of this Pullman train, and it must be said that the earlier decision to paint it in BR livery after sixty years in umber and cream, when it was known to have only a few years to go, showed gross insensitivity. Anyway, on the day, in addition to the three timetabled runs each way, there was an extra up run at 18.50 for a wine and cheese party (£7.50), and an extra down run at 22.30 for a "Champagne Special" (£10). Finally on 9th May there was a "musical excursion", also with champagne. There was also great concern at rumours that all three trains were to be sold to America, though in the event all cars were sold as separate items and bought by UK people. In October 1972 five "Golden Arrow" Pullmans were offered for sale, Nos. 301/2, 306–8. They were moved from Stewarts Lane depot to Lovers Walk, Brighton, where they joined some unsold "Brighton Belle" cars, though some of these had already left in an undignified way by freight train, as No. 288 did via Norwood and Temple Mills to Clacton. Cars 285–7 and 291–3 were bought as a block by Allied Breweries, but were destined to spend some twelve months in sidings first as Mistley and then at Manningtree.

This was not, of course, the end of Pullman nationwide, though after 1978 the only regular train running was the "Manchester Pullman". On 13th September, 1979 a train commemorating the centenary of the dining car included the Pullmans *Eagle*, *Emerald* and, as mentioned above, *Topaz* (I). A Pullman breakfast car was put on the Harwich–Manchester train in the summer of 1979, and there were dozens of private "Belle" trains running around using preserved cars. In 1983 named Pullmans returned with refurbished stock on the Manchester Pullman, and in 1985 a new "Pullman" train was made up using standard Mk IIIb InterCity stock. Moreover the idea, if not the name, remained in the introduction in 1984 of an "Executive Saloon" which could be put into an InterCity 125 train for an "excess fare" of £200! However, all these vehicles might be called "Pullman", but the real heirs were the preserved trains in umber-and-cream livery, described in the next chapter.

Perhaps the best evidence of the indestructibility of the Pullman Idea is an advertisement by BR in February 1986: "We have reintroduced the famous Pullman train": 22 new luxury coaches on 24 workings to the north and north-east. Will there ever be a new "Brighton Belle"? Who knows.

TABLE THREE — PULLMAN CARS COMING TO SR LINES AFTER 1927 LIST (p.x.)

Adrian	1928 K O	*Lady Dalziel*	1930 Bk G
Alice	1932 K C B	*Loraine*	1928 K O
Anne	1932 K C B	*Lorna*	1932 K C B
Aquilla	1951 K G G	*Lucille*	1928 P L
Aries	1951 K GG		
Audrey	1932 K B	*Maid of Kent* (II)[2]	
		May	1932 K C B
Bertha	1932 K C B	*Mona*	1932 K B
Brenda	1932 K C B		
		Naomi	1932 K C B
Carina	1951 K GG		
Clara	1932 K C B	*Olive*	1932 K C B
Cygnus	1951 P GG	*Onyx*	1932 K C B
		Orion	1951 K GG
Daisy	1932 K C B		
Diamond	1928 K G	*Pearl*	1924 K G
Doris	1932 K B	*Peggy*	1932 K C B
		Pegasus	1951 Bar GG
Elinor	1932 K C B	*Penelope*	1928 P L
Enid	1932 K C B	*Perseus*	1951 P GG
Ethel	1932 K C B	*Phyllis*	1928 P L
Eunice	1928 P G	*Philomel*	1928 P L
Evadne	1928 K O	*Phoenix*	1951 P GG[3]
		Princess Elizabeth	1930 P B L O
Grace	1932 K C B		
Gwladys	1932 K C B	*Rainbow* (II)[4]	
Gwen	1932 K B	*Rita*	1932 K C B
		Rose	1932 K C B
Hazel	1932 K B	*Ruth*	1932 K C B
Hercules	1951 P GG		
		Ursula	1928 P L
Ida	1932 K C B		
Ione	1928 K G	*Vera*	1932 K B
Iris	1932 K C B	*Violet*	1932 K C B
Isle of Thanet[1]			
		Zena	1928 P O
Joan	1928 P O		
Joyce	1932 K C B		
Juana	1928 P O		

"Brighton Belle" sets were:

3051: 88 *Hazel*   *Doris* 86 89
3052: 90 *Vera*   *Audrey* 87 91
3053: 92 *Gwen*   *Mona* 85 93

Third/Second Class Cars

No. 40	(1921) Bk P W LE	No. 96	see *Sylvia*
No. 41	(1920) Bk P W LE	No. 97	see *Calais*
No. 45	(1920) K L 12	No. 98	see *Milan*
No. 47	(1920) K L 12	No. 99	see *Padua*
No. 54	(1923) Bk P LE	No. 132	see *Anaconda*
No. 55	(1923) Bk P LE	No. 133	see *Erminie*
No. 60	(1925) K W	No. 135	see *Elmira*
No. 61	(1925) K LE	No. 137	see *Maid of Kent* II
No. 63	(1925) Bk P LE	No. 153	see *Aurora*
No. 65	(1925) K LE	No. 154	see *Flora*
No. 75	(1928) P L	No. 161	see *Fortuna* (K ex-ER)
No. 76	(1928) P L	No. 162	see *Irene* (K ex-ER)
No. 81	(1931) Bk P W	No. 166	see *Geraldine*
No. 82	(1931) Bk P L W	No. 167	see *Marjorie*
No. 83	(1931) P W	No. 169	see *Viking*
No. 84	(1931) P L W	No. 171	see *Pauline*
No. 85–7	(1932) P B	No. 181–5	ex-Hastings cars, see text
No. 88–93	(1982) M Bk P B	No. 194	see Car 36
No. 94	(1920) Bk P 12 ex-ER *Ansonia*	No. 208	see *Leona*
		No. 248	see *Lady Dalziel*
No. 95	(1920) Bk P 12 ex-ER *Arcadia*	No. 249	see *Pearl*
		No. 303	new 1952, K GG

NOTES

K	–	kitchen or buffet	W	–	1931 "Bournemouth Belle"
P	–	parlour	B	–	1932 Brighton electric
Bk	–	brake or guard	O	–	ex-GWR cars, 1930
M	–	motored	G	–	1928 "Golden Arrow"
C	–	composite	GG	–	1951 "Golden Arrow"
			L	–	ex-LNER 1928 all-steel
			LE	–	earlier ex-LNER

[1] *Isle of Thanet* renaming of *Princess Elizabeth*.
[2] *Maid of Kent* II renaming of *Formosa*.
[3] *Phoenix* reconstruction of *Rainbow* I.
[4] *Rainbow* II renaming of *Cosmo Bonsor*.

Believed cars 34–6 ran for a time as 192–4 (2nd class).

Some other cars appear in records as second class but no photograph of a car lettered "Second Class" is known.

Emerald was renumbered Second Class Car No. 1 about 1944, later instruction car 101.

Juno and *Aurora* briefly carried second class Nos. 502/3 in 1950.

Chapter Ten
The Preservation Era

As already stated, the preservation of Pullman cars began well before the last ran in public service on the SR lines; however, few can have foreseen the extent of the Pullman activity to follow. At the core of this were three trains; one was the Sea Containers Ltd Venice–Simplon–Orient Express (VSOE), the UK arm of which ran from Victoria to Folkestone, hauled by BR locomotives though the stock was privately-owned. This first ran regularly from 28th May, 1982, and was made up from a variety of fairly old cars, refurbished at Steamtown Carnforth; some had been purchased direct and some obtained from static exhibition. The down train ran on Fridays and Saturdays, and the up arrived on Sundays and Thursdays; a third trip was added for a time, but there seemed to be scope for hiring too as the train was seen on race and other Specials. The original cars were three 1951 "Golden Arrow" cars. *Cygnus*, *Carina* and *Perseus*, one ex-"Brighton Belle" car *Audrey*, and some 1925–8 cars *Ibis*, *Phoenix*, *Minerva* and *Zena*. *Phoenix* and *Carina* had crossed the Channel in March 1973 and spent some years as restaurants at Lyons, before returning. A baggage car made up from an LNER pigeon van completed the train.

The second train, the Bulmer's Cider Train, has already been mentioned. The third was that run by the Steam Locomotive Operators' Association from a base at Carlisle. In collaboration with BR this train ran steam excursions all over the system; however, there were no ex-SR cars in it, since the whole train of eight cars was from the 1960 ER steel-bodied stock, purchased in 1981. In 1983 the train was sold to Flying Scotsman Enterprises.

In addition to these trains, there were other cars making public runs; the Kent & East Sussex Railway made great use of their Hastings cars *Theodora* and *Barbara*, and built another "Pullman" out of a BR restaurant car, named *Diana*. Specials included one in 1981 to celebrate the 150th anniversary of the birth of G. M. Pullman.

Film companies also sought the period atmosphere lent by genuine Pullman cars. In November 1975 a film called "Agatha" was being made at Scarborough, and required a Pullman train. *Topaz* was lent by the National Railway Museum, *Zena* and *Rosalind* came from Carnforth where they were then located, and *Perseus* and *Cygnus* from the North Yorkshire Moors Railway; the last-named carried the name *Anne* on one side only for the film for some reason.

Not all "preserved" Pullmans led uneventful lives. After initial "panic buying" of the older cars to make sure they did not get

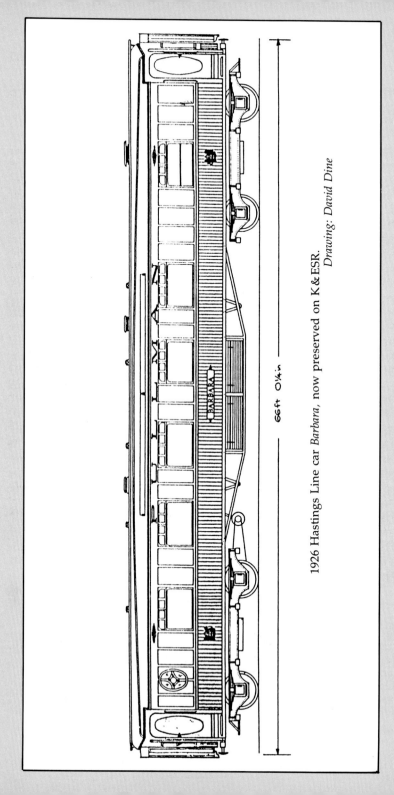

1926 Hastings Line car *Barbara*, now preserved on K&ESR.

Drawing: David Dine

scrapped, some swopping, buying and lending took place, resulting in cars moving long distances by rail or road. *Agatha* and *Fingall*, after their short stay at the Beaulieu Museum, crossed to the Isle of Wight, but seven years later returned back across the water to serve the Orient Express and the Bluebell Railway respectively. *Topaz* (I), restored by the Pullman Co. in 1961 for preservation, had most of the inside torn out again in 1979 to serve as an exhibition saloon in the touring train commemorating the centenary of the dining car, and in 1986 was "restored" again, this time in the original 1913 lake livery. Some were genuinely static and may remain so, though a few clocked up short mileages: *Doris* took time off from duty as a businessman's dining room at Finchley Road station to visit Derby in 1975 for re-painting in original livery. *Orion* went to Wolverton for a similar purpose in 1978; *Aurora* and *Alicante* did the short trip from Fowey to Marazion in 1964 when WR camping coaches were concentrated at that place.

The two "Devon Belle" observation cars had perhaps the most varied lives of all. It will be recalled that they had originally been ambulance cars on the LNWR in 1918, converted to Pullmans in 1921, and rebuilt as bar cars in 1937. In 1946 they were remodelled as observation cars, and were sold in 1957 to BR. No. 14 was put on the Glasgow–Oban run as Sc281. No. 13 became M280 and was on the North Wales Land Cruise, later (1961) going to Scotland as Sc280 on the Kyle of Lochalsh line, being joined there in 1967 by No. 14. No. 14 was sold again in 1969 and went overseas with the "USA Flying Scotsman", ending up as a club in California. No. 13 was sold to the Torbay Railway for service on the Paignton line restored to Pullman livery; it has also worked on the associated Dart Valley line. Both cars seem to have carried BR livery in Scotland, though one was noted on excursions in the mid-sixties in a livery similar to Pullman but with BR logos and a long white stripe along the side, which it had also carried when owned by Pullman, with the words "Pullman Observation Car" painted on it. No. 13 is now the oldest Pullman car in regular service, since the three older cars which have been preserved are static.

TABLE FOUR — FORMER SR AND BR(S) PULLMANS PRESERVED

Pre-1923 cars

Alicante	Marazion from 1964, before that at Fowey as Holiday Coach.
Elmira	R&ER Ravenglass: previously Car 135.
Emerald (I)	Conwy Valley Museum
Mimosa	Marazion
Rosalind	VSOE from 1980; before that Steamtown Carnforth.

Sapphire	Ashford Steam Centre, then Lavender Line, Isfield, Surrey.
Topaz (I)	National Railway Museum from 1960; previously pres. Pullman Co.

Pre-1951 cars (steam-hauled)

Agatha	Beaulieu Museum, then Wight Rly, 1980 to VSOE.
Aurora	Marazion, before 1964 at Fowey, Holiday Coach.
Barbara	KESR Tenterden
Fingall	Beaulieu Museum, then Wight Rly, 1980 to Bluebell Rly.
Flora	Marazion
Ibis	VSOE; previously Birmingham Transport Museum.
Ione	VSOE, before that Birmingham Transport Museum.
Isle of Thanet	Wisconsin USA
Joan	Wisconsin USA
Juno	Marazion
Lucille	Ashford Steam Centre, then to VSOE 1985.
Lydia	Wisconsin USA
Maid of Kent (I)	R&ER Ravenglass; Car 137 from 1948.
Maid of Kent (II)	Privately, Kings Lynn.
Malaga	Messrs Ian Allan Shepperton
Minerva	VSOE; previously Lytham Museum.
Montana	Privately
Phyllis	Ashford Steam Centre
Theodora	KESR Tenterden
Ursula	Pub., Hilderstone, Staffs.
Zena	VSOE from 1980, before that Birmingham Transpor. Museum.

Car No. 13	Dart Valley/Torbay Rly (ex-Observations Cars)
Car No. 14	San Francisco USA (ex-Observation Cars)
Car No. 36	Bulmer Cider Train, then to VSOE 1986
Car No. 54	VSOE; previously Birmingham Transport Museum, now to Bluebell.
Car No. 75	Pub., Hilderstone Staffs.
Car No. 83	Bulmer Cider Train, then to VSOE 1986.
Car No. 84	Keighley & Worth Valley Rly
Car No. 97	(*Calais*); Marazion.
Car No. 99	(*Padua*); VSOE, before that Steamtown Carnforth.
Car No. 208	Privately

Pre-1951 cars (electric)

Of the 6-PUL composites only two are preserved; *Bertha* on Bluebell Rly (Mid-Hants Rly until 1982); *Ruth* in Bulmers Centre.

All the "Brighton Belle" cars were sold, but some have moved around since; of six cars bought by Allied Breweries, only one in the end served a public house use, three passing to private railways and two to Brighton Museum. 279 *Hazel*, 283 *Mona*, 285 became public house adjuncts in various places; 280 *Audrey* after a time in private hands went to VSOE; 281 *Gwen* to Colne Valley Rly; 287, 291 North Norfolk Rly; 290 Nene Valley Rly but operated by BR as a bar car; 288 to Stour Valley Rly and in 1981 to Swanage Rly; 282 *Doris* became a business man's private dining room in Finchley Road sidings; 292/3 returned to Brighton 1976 from storage on ER for the Transport Museum at Preston Park.

1951 "Golden Arrow" Cars

Of the ten cars, at least eight are preserved. *Perseus* and *Cygnus* went first to the North Yorkshire Moors Rly and in 1979 to VSOE; *Aquila* to Bulmers Cider Train, then to VSOE 1986; *Phoenix* and *Carina* went first to Lyons France, but came back in 1980 for VSOE; *Pegasus* went to Birmingham Transport Museum; *Aries* became a pub at Rochdale; *Orion* went to a static role in a replica station at Beer, Devon. Only *Hercules* and Car 303 do not seem to have survived.

In the above VSOE stands for Venice–Simplon–Orient Express (see text); Marazion is where WR holiday coaches were moved in 1964 for staff use.

The precise ending of every Pullman car cannot be determined. A few saw some use as service vehicles after a camping career. A few more had their bodies grounded in the thirties, at Partridge Green, Selsey, Bishopstone and other places where such bungalows abounded, and it is possible some survive. It is believed that two short cars, which spent most of their life on the Highland Railway and were built into a house at Seaford, Sussex in the twenties, are still there though, apart from a fit of idleness at Brighton, they were never on the SR. It may be asked why, since a Pullman made a better house than a compartment carriage, more were not so used. Two possible answers are that by the time cars were being withdrawn around 1930 the peak of carriage-houses had passed; also that the bodies were heavy and long, and means for conveying them by road for anything but short distances did not then exist. Now, in the preservation era, Pullmans have made long journeys by road and sea, and no doubt will continue to do so as the fortunes of the private railways on which they now serve ebb and flow.

TABLE FIVE — DISPOSITION OF PULLMAN CARS, 1874–1974

	MR	*GNR*	*LCDR*	*LBSCR*	*LSWR*	*HR*	*SECR*	*CAL*	*GER*	*MET*	*GWR*	*SR*	*LNER*	*LMS*	*GS(I)*	*Total*
1874	5	–	–	–	–	–	–	–	–	–						5
1883	28	5	1	7	–	–	–	–	–	–						41
1890	*	2	–	12	2	2	–	–	–	–						18
1900		2	–	21	4	2	–	–	–	–						25
1910		*	–	32	2	2	10	–	–	2						48
1914			–	36	–	–	23	10	–	2						71
1922				54	–	–	56	18	15	2						145
1929										2	7	141	67	24	4	245
1933										2	–	155	68	*	4	229
1939										2	–	147	54	–	4	207
1946											–	145	53	–		198
1952											–	165	43	–		208
1955											10	141	43	–		194
1960											34	119	87	12		252
1967											36	34	44	29		143
1974											–	–	44	29		71

Notes:

Approximate numbers of Pullman cars available on various lines during years shown.

* cars continued in use but in railway ownership.

A reader attempting to compare the totals with the progressive numbering of cars in the "Schedule", should remember that cars not still on the strength by 1915 were not included, also that numbering in the Schedule did not run strictly in date order.

Although the numbers given above are as nearly correct as possible, the "pooling" of cars, particularly between the LNER and SR in later years, could slightly affect the figures.

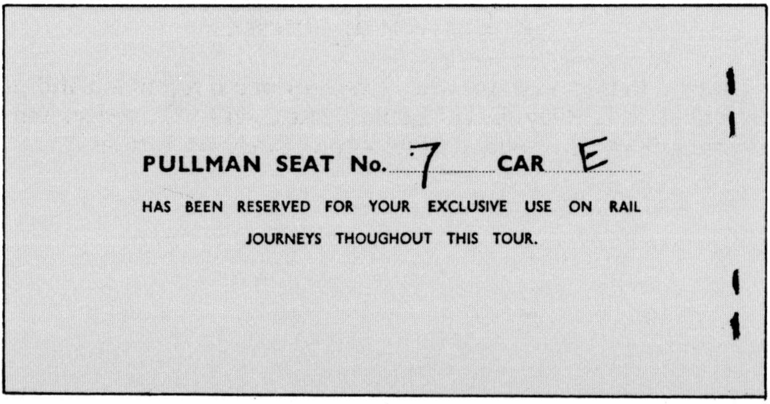
PULLMAN SEAT No. 7 CAR E

HAS BEEN RESERVED FOR YOUR EXCLUSIVE USE ON RAIL JOURNEYS THOUGHOUT THIS TOUR.

Bibliography

Pullman & Perfection by F. Burtt and W. Beckerlegge (Ian Allan 1948) gives a brief survey of the history of Pullmans, a list of all extant cars and of cars by that time out of service.

Pullman by Julian Morel (David & Charles 1983) is written by a former officer of the Company and is very good on organisation and personnel, with less detail on the trains, but does have a complete list of the 1960 "schedule" numbers, and of preserved cars.

History of Trains de Luxe by George Behrend (Transport Publishing Co. 1977) is mostly about wagons-lits activities on the Continent, but the list of world-wide Pullman cars covers the UK in detail as regards rebuildings etc.

Magazine Articles: there is a distinct and surprising lack of authentic articles on Pullmans at any date: *The Railway Magazine* in early days largely ignored them, though the *Locomotive Magazine* mentioned the introduction of some batches of new cars. The following articles have provided some material, more having come from brief mentions too numerous to list:

The Brighton Limited, *Locomotive Magazine,* 15th May, 1951 p.76.

SER All-Car Trains, *Locomotive Magazine,* 15th April, 1952 p.59.

The Southern Belle, *Railway Magazine,* July 1935, p.62.

The Bournemouth Belle, *Meccano Magazine,* 1931, p.708.

G. M. Pullman Centenary, *Railway Magazine,* May 1931, p.379.

The New "Golden Arrow", *Railway Gazette,* 8th June, 1951, p.638.

Belle Trains, *Railway Magazine,* May, 1972.

Pullman Cars on the SECR, *Railway Magazine,* 1910 (1), p.409.

Pullman Cars, *Locomotive Magazine,* 5th January, 1924, p.11.

New Pullman Cars for Brighton & Worthing, *Locomotive Magazine,* 14th January, 1933.

Acknowledgements

Grateful thanks to those who have provided information and particularly to R.C. Riley, David Gould, J. Kent, H.C. Casserley, and to the publishers for providing photocopies of elusive articles.

THE PULLMAN CAR COMPANY, LTD.

Pullman Drawing Room, Buffet, Dining and Observation Cars are in operation on the following important lines—

SOUTHERN RAILWAY. Victoria and London Bridge to Brighton, Hove, Worthing Eastbourne, Bognor, Newhaven, Portsmouth, etc.
Victoria and Charing Cross to Dover and Folkestone in all the Continental Services. Also Hastings, Deal, Ramsgate, Margate, and Kent Coast Towns.
Waterloo and Southampton and Bournemouth also Waterloo and Southampton Docks in connection with Ocean Liners.

LONDON & NORTH EASTERN. First and Third Class Pullman Trains from King's Cross to Leeds, Harrogate, Darlington, Newcastle, Drem, Edinburgh, and Glasgow. Also to Leeds, Halifax, Bradford, Wakefield, Harrogate, Ripon, Darlington and Newcastle.
Buffet Cars (First Class) from Liverpool Street on Continental Trains connecting with Hook of Holland and Antwerp and Flushing.

LONDON MIDLAND AND SCOTTISH. Dining Cars from Glasgow and Edinburgh to Aberdeen, Oban, Perth, Stirling, Gleneagles, Dunblane, Forfar, Callander, Lockerbie, Loch Awe, Carstairs, Beattock, Carlisle, etc.. Blair Atholl, Newtonmore, Kingussie, Kincraig, Aviemore, etc.

METROPOLITAN. Buffet Cars are run between Aldgate, Liverpool Street, Baker Street, Aylesbury, Chesham, and Verney Junction.

GREAT SOUTHERN RLYS. OF IRELAND. Buffet Cars are run between Dublin and Cork, Dublin and Limerick, and Dublin and Sligo.

"The Southern Belle."

Daily (including Sundays). Pullman Train de Luxe. Running between LONDON AND BRIGHTON.

The most Luxurious Train in the World.

"QUEEN OF SCOTS."

Pullman Limited Train. Daily (Sundays excepted). Between London, Leeds, Harrogate, Darlington, Newcastle, Drem (for North Berwick), Edinburgh and Glasgow.

"WEST RIDING" PULLMAN LIMITED TRAIN.

Daily (Sundays excepted). Between London, Wakefield, Leeds, Bradford, Halifax, Harrogate, Ripon, Darlington, and Newcastle.

HARROGATE SUNDAY PULLMAN.

Between London, Leeds, Bradford and Harrogate.

"GOLDEN ARROW."

Between London (Victoria) and Paris.

PULLMAN TRAINS ARE RUN TO MOST OF THE PRINCIPAL RACE MEETINGS.

"THE EASTERN BELLE," LTD. From Liverpool Street Station to Clacton every Sunday during Summer Months, and East Coast Resorts on week-days.

"THE BOURNEMOUTH BELLE." First and Third Class between London (Waterloo) and Southampton and Bournemouth.

Refreshments.	Breakfasts, Luncheons, Teas, Dinners, and other refreshments can be obtained on the Cars.
Reservations.	Reservations, with certain exceptions, can be effected through the Station Superintendents at the various termini, either by letter, telegram, or telephone.
Special Facilities.	Cars for private parties can be specially reserved, under certain conditions, upon application to the various Railway Companies.

THE PULLMAN CAR COMPANY, LTD.

Chief London Office :

VICTORIA STATION (SOUTHERN RAILWAY, EASTERN SECTION), PIMLICO, S.W.1.

Telegraphic Address—"Pullman, Rail, London." Telephone No.—Victoria 9978 (2 lines).
Branch Office—KINGSBRIDGE STATION, DUBLIN. Telephone No.—Dublin 23114.
Branch Office—CENTRAL STATION (London Midland and Scottish Railway), GLASGOW. Telephone No.—Central 2043.

Advertisement from *Railway Year Book,* 1934